THE ULTIMATE BARNDOMINIUM MASTERPLAN

MASTERPLAN

A STEP-BY-STEP GUIDE WITH VISUAL BLUEPRINTS, BUDGETING TOOLS, AND SUCCESS STORIES TO BUILD YOUR CUSTOM, ENERGY-EFFICIENT HOME RIGHT—WITHOUT BREAKING THE BANK

COLE BENNETT

COPYRIGHT

CONTENTS

1. DREAM IT RIGHT 7
   The Rise of the Barndominium Lifestyle: Freedom, Affordability, and Functionality 7
   Real-World Stories of Couples, Families, and DIYers Who Made the Leap 8
   What Makes a Barndominium Different from a Traditional Home (and Why It Matters) 8
   How to Visualize Your Future Home, Lifestyle, and Land Needs 9
   A Self-Assessment: Are You Ready to Build Your Own Barndominium? 9

2. PLAN WITHOUT PANIC 11
   Choosing the Right Land: Utilities, Access, Orientation, and Zoning 11
   Understanding Permits and County Codes: What Most Builders Forget to Tell You 12
   How to Design for Real Life: Layout Planning That Matches the Way You Actually Live 13
   Visual Floor Plans with Annotations: From Cozy to Colossal 14
   Customizing Your Layout: Tools, Space-Planning Hacks, and Multipurpose Design 42
   Budget Planning Tools and Timelines (with a Downloadable Worksheet) 44

3. BUILD SMART, SPEND LESS 48
   Materials That Last — and Those That Cost More Than They're Worth 48
   Budgeting Your Build: Realistic Examples and Contractor Red Flags 50
   GC or DIY? How to Decide and What to Expect From Both. 53
   Visual Construction Timeline: What Happens When and in What Order 55
   Energy Efficiency Systems: HVAC, Insulation, Solar, Water 58
   Off-Grid Options and Passive Design for Long-Term Savings 61
   The "$25K Mistake" Checklist: Critical Steps You Can't Afford to Miss 63

4. FINISH STRONG, LIVE FREE 66
   Interior Finishes: Rustic, Modern, or a Blend of Both 66
   Passing Inspection: What They'll Check and How to Prepare 73
   Real Success Stories: What Real Barndominium Owners Learned the Hard Way 75
   Long-Term Maintenance and Upgrades to Protect Your Investment 78
   How to Make Your Barndominium Feel Like Home From Day One 80
   A Look Forward: Legacy Living, Resale Value, and Financial Freedom 81

Glossary 85
About the author 87

CHAPTER 1
DREAM IT RIGHT

Why Barndominiums Are Booming and How to Know If It's Right for You

There's a quiet revolution happening in American homebuilding—one that trades drywall palaces for durability, efficiency, and function-first design. Barndominiums, once considered niche or alternative housing, have rapidly evolved into a mainstream solution for individuals and families who are ready to build smarter, not just bigger. But beneath the trending hashtags and social media snapshots, there's a deeper truth: barndominiums aren't just about style—they're about solving real-world problems with practical design and long-term flexibility.

This chapter isn't about convincing you to follow a fad. It's about taking a hard, informed look at why thousands of Americans are turning to steel or post-frame construction for their primary homes, workshops, or legacy properties. As someone who has spent years in the field—from excavation to finish carpentry—I've seen firsthand how the barndo model solves critical lifestyle and financial challenges in ways conventional construction can't.

If you're here because you want creative control, long-term value, or the ability to live and work from the same footprint, you're in the right place. But before a shovel hits the ground, you need to make sure this path truly aligns with your goals, your land, and your life. Let's start by getting honest about what makes this approach work—and what doesn't.

THE RISE OF THE BARNDOMINIUM LIFESTYLE: FREEDOM, AFFORDABILITY, AND FUNCTIONALITY

The growth of the barndominium lifestyle isn't accidental—it's a direct response to the limitations of traditional housing models. Homeowners are increasingly rejecting high-maintenance suburban builds, inflated square footage that serves no practical purpose, and the long-term financial burden of thirty-year mortgages tied to inefficient structures. In their place, a new kind of dwelling has emerged—one that prioritizes utility, long-term sustainability, and the freedom to adapt a space to fit real human needs.

Barndominiums, or "barndos," appeal to a demographic that values space efficiency over vanity square footage. These aren't just barn-shaped houses—they're intelligently designed, highly functional homes that integrate shop space, storage, and livable square footage under one roof. Whether you're running a small business from your garage, parking a tractor under your kitchen window, or raising a family with access to wide-open rural land, the barndominium model offers a structural framework that flexes to meet those needs.

What has driven this movement isn't just cost—it's control. Barndominiums give owners more say in how their home functions, how it grows, and how it serves their lifestyle. This model has taken root in areas where practicality trumps pretense, and where people want homes that are as hard-working and versatile as they are.

REAL-WORLD STORIES OF COUPLES, FAMILIES, AND DIYERS WHO MADE THE LEAP

One of the most compelling aspects of the barndominium movement is that it isn't driven by corporations, developers, or big-budget HGTV fantasies. It's powered by real people—working families, independent couples, and hands-on DIYers—who've stepped outside the traditional path of homeownership and built something that fits the way they actually live.

Take the Millers, for example—a retired couple from eastern Oklahoma who sold their suburban home and built a 1,600-square-foot barndo with an attached 1,000-square-foot shop. Their goal was simple: live closer to their grandkids, reduce their monthly expenses, and never have to deal with a homeowners' association again. With metal siding, spray foam insulation, and a south-facing roof ready for solar, they now live in a home that costs less to operate and gives them more functional freedom than they ever had before.

Then there's the Ramirez family in central Texas. As a blended family of six, they needed bedrooms for the kids, office space for remote work, and a large open-concept area to gather—on a budget. Rather than sacrifice space or location, they bought five acres outside city limits and built a custom barndo that delivered all three. Their garage doubles as a homeschool room and woodworking studio, and the design allows them to expand later without disrupting the core of the home.

And finally, people like Jeremy—a single firefighter in Arkansas who took on much of his own build over weekends and holidays. With basic framing experience and a few trusted subcontractors, he created a compact, efficient barndo that includes living quarters, a workshop, and covered parking for his off-road vehicles. He saved over $60,000 compared to a conventional build—and gained a structure designed specifically around how he lives, not how a developer thinks he should.

These stories vary in scope, but the common thread is control. These aren't show homes; they're **smart homes**—not in the tech sense, but in the way they reflect the values, goals, and lifestyles of the people who built them.

WHAT MAKES A BARNDOMINIUM DIFFERENT FROM A TRADITIONAL HOME (AND WHY IT MATTERS)

At first glance, a barndominium might resemble a conventional house with a rural twist—but structurally and functionally, the differences run deep. These aren't just aesthetic variations; they are core design and construction principles that shift how the home is built, lived in, and maintained over time.

The most immediate distinction is the **structural system**. While traditional homes typically rely on stick-framing with load-bearing interior walls, a barndominium—especially one built on a steel or post-frame foundation—uses **clear-span construction**. This means that the internal space is largely free of load-bearing walls, allowing for open-concept layouts, flexible room placement, and future reconfigurations without major structural changes. It's not just a design trend—it's a building strategy that reduces material waste, speeds up framing, and cuts labor costs.

Secondly, **barndos are engineered for durability**. With metal roofing and siding as standard, these structures outperform conventional homes in terms of weather resistance, pest control, and lifespan. Steel framing resists rot, mold, and termites. Maintenance cycles are longer and less costly, which matters significantly for owners living in remote or rural environments where service calls aren't a phone call away.

Functionality is another major differentiator. Traditional homes often separate garage, storage, and living functions, leading to inefficiencies in space and flow. Barndominiums integrate these elements by design. A barndo's garage isn't just for vehicles—it's often a workshop, a business space, or even a second living area. This **multi-purpose approach** reflects the evolving needs of homeowners who aren't just looking for shelter —they're looking for a space that supports how they work, create, and live.

Finally, the economics of a barndominium make it fundamentally different. These builds typically offer **lower cost-per-square-foot ratios**, not only because of reduced materials and faster build times, but because they focus on usable space over architectural fluff. You're not paying for vaulted foyers or formal dining rooms you'll never use—you're investing in square footage that works as hard as you do.

Understanding these differences isn't just academic—it's foundational to making informed decisions about your future home. Choosing a barndominium isn't about choosing a style. It's about choosing a **system of building** that prioritizes strength, flexibility, and value in every square inch.

HOW TO VISUALIZE YOUR FUTURE HOME, LIFESTYLE, AND LAND NEEDS

Before a floor plan is drawn or a site is cleared, successful barndominium builds begin with a clear, grounded vision—not just of the structure, but of how that structure will support your life. In my years as a builder, I've seen one consistent factor that separates well-executed barndominiums from those that fall short: the owners took the time to think in terms of **function over form**. They didn't just imagine what their home would *look* like—they understood how it needed to *work*.

Start by picturing your **daily routine**. How do you enter the home? Do you come through a garage, a mudroom, or straight through the front door with work boots on? Where do the kids drop their backpacks, where does laundry get sorted, and where do tools or outdoor gear get stored? These questions help shape not only the floor plan but the **entire orientation of the house** on your land.

Speaking of land—don't underestimate its impact. Your barndominium's layout should respond to your site conditions, not fight them. Pay attention to **natural slope, sun exposure, and prevailing wind**. A south-facing rear porch might give you shade in the summer and warmth in the winter. Proper siting also affects utilities—are you hauling in water, running septic, or tying into a municipal grid? These factors should inform your home's footprint and the type of systems you'll need from day one.

Then consider your **lifestyle over time**. Are you planning for aging in place, future expansion, or a business run out of the shop space? A barndominium's strength is in its adaptability, but only if you plan for it early. Structural overbuilds—like leaving trusses open in the garage or roughing in plumbing for a future bath—can save thousands later when your needs change.

Lastly, get visual. Don't rely on abstract ideas. Print floor plans. Sketch traffic flow. Tape off room dimensions in your current garage or yard. I've had clients mark out living spaces with landscaping flags just to get a feel for how a 30x60 layout lives in real space. It's one thing to see a plan on paper—it's another to physically walk it and sense the proportions.

This isn't about dreaming small or big. It's about dreaming *clearly*. The better you can visualize the flow of your life inside the structure you're building, the fewer compromises you'll make, and the fewer costly changes you'll face during construction. Build your vision before you build your walls.

A SELF-ASSESSMENT: ARE YOU READY TO BUILD YOUR OWN BARNDOMINIUM?

Before you commit to building a barndominium, you need to step back—not from the blueprints or budget sheets, but from your own expectations. Building a home, especially one as hands-on and customizable as a barndo, isn't just a construction project. It's a test of mindset, patience, and long-term vision. I've seen clients succeed beyond their expectations—and I've seen others struggle—not because of materials or mistakes, but because they weren't fully prepared for what this kind of build demands.

Start by assessing your **goals**. Why are you drawn to this type of home? If your answer is purely aesthetic, that's not enough. A barndominium offers far more than looks—it's about function, flexibility, and long-term value. If you're after a living space that works as hard as you do, that grows with your needs, and that saves money over time rather than up front, then you're thinking like a builder, not just a buyer.

Next, be honest about your **tolerance for decision-making**. Unlike buying a pre-built house, you'll be making calls on everything from foundation type to door swing direction. Even if you're working with a contractor, the design and oversight will require your input. This isn't a passive process—and indecision is one of the most expensive delays on any build.

Evaluate your **budget realism**. Not just how much you can spend, but how much you're willing to research, plan, and potentially compromise to stay on track. Cost control in barndominium builds comes from understanding trade-offs—knowing where to invest (insulation, roofing, foundation) and where to economize without cutting corners. Are you prepared to stick to your plan when prices shift or delays happen?

Finally, think about your **problem-solving capacity**. Every build encounters obstacles—weather, permitting issues, subcontractor no-shows. If your default reaction is to panic or point fingers, this may not be the right time to build. But if you're ready to face issues with flexibility and focus—if you see challenges as opportunities to refine rather than derail—then you're likely ready for the process ahead.

Building a barndominium is not for everyone. But for those who come in prepared—mentally, financially, and practically—it's one of the most rewarding forms of homeownership available today. If your answers to these questions reveal gaps, that's not a dealbreaker. It's a starting point. Use this book as your framework, your fallback, and your guide. You don't have to know everything now. You just have to be willing to learn as you go—and to commit to the build like you plan to live in it.

CHAPTER 2
PLAN WITHOUT PANIC

Land, Laws, Layouts, and Logistics—All the Things You Need to Know Before You Build

Before the first truck shows up with framing materials or a permit is pulled from the county office, there's groundwork that has nothing to do with concrete—and everything to do with clarity. Planning is where most barndominium builds succeed or fail, and not because of what people don't know, but because of what they assume they already do.

This chapter is designed to eliminate guesswork and replace it with strategy. We're going to cover what you really need to understand before building begins—starting with land selection, moving into legal considerations, and finally, aligning your layout and logistics with how you plan to live in the space. No vague advice, no recycled Pinterest tips—just field-tested insight from real builds that have gone right, and a few that didn't.

Whether you're hiring a general contractor or managing this yourself, the same principle applies: **your build is only as strong as your plan.** Let's make sure yours is rock solid.

CHOOSING THE RIGHT LAND: UTILITIES, ACCESS, ORIENTATION, AND ZONING

Selecting your land isn't just the first step in your barndominium journey—it's the foundation on which every decision after this will rest. And I mean that literally. The wrong property can turn a well-planned build into a logistical nightmare, while the right one can make the entire process smoother, more affordable, and more aligned with your long-term goals. Too often, people choose land based on price or scenery alone. That's a mistake. This decision needs to be technical.

Start with **access**. You'll need to ensure there's a legally deeded road or easement to the property. This might sound obvious, but I've seen plenty of people get tied up in right-of-way disputes that stalled their build by months. And even if access exists, consider the quality—can construction vehicles navigate it safely? Will you need to grade it or lay gravel before the first delivery arrives?

Next is **utilities**. Is there existing electric service nearby, or will you need to bring in poles and transformers? How close is the nearest water line—or are you on your own with a well? Septic feasibility should be verified early, especially in areas with shallow soil or high water tables. Don't rely on a seller's assurances—get a perc test and speak directly with your local health department.

Orientation matters more than many realize. Positioning your home with the sun, wind, and slope in mind can dramatically improve energy efficiency and comfort. A southern-facing rear elevation, for instance, allows for passive solar gain in winter and shaded evenings in summer. Natural breezeways can help cool the home without relying on HVAC systems. Use topography to your advantage—don't fight the land, work with it.

And then there's **zoning and permitting**, which can vary wildly from one county—or even one township—to the next. Some jurisdictions are barndominium-friendly, others treat them as unconventional builds requiring variances or additional engineering. Know your local building authority's stance before you commit. Verify minimum square footage requirements, height restrictions, easements, floodplain data, and setbacks. It's also smart to check whether the land is in an agricultural, residential, or mixed-use zone—each comes with different allowances and limits.

Finally, consider your **lifestyle priorities**. Will you need a second structure for a shop or home business? Do you plan to homestead, raise animals, or go off-grid in the future? Your land should accommodate not just what you're building now, but what you may build later.

Buying land is not about buying what's pretty. It's about buying what works—for your build, your location, and your long-term lifestyle. Make this decision like a builder, not a dreamer. That's how you prevent surprises and protect your investment before the first stake goes in the ground.

UNDERSTANDING PERMITS AND COUNTY CODES: WHAT MOST BUILDERS FORGET TO TELL YOU

If there's one part of this process that catches more first-time builders off guard than any other, it's the permitting phase. Unlike choosing finishes or laying out your floor plan, this isn't the part you get to personalize—but it is the part you **must get right**. And unfortunately, this is also where many people assume "it'll work itself out," only to face red tape, delays, fines, or worse: a total stop order from the county.

The first thing to understand is that **barndominiums are not universally defined or accepted** by all building authorities. Some counties treat them like any other single-family dwelling. Others classify them as accessory structures or non-standard builds—especially if you're using steel framing, post-frame construction, or combining a residence with shop space under the same roof. This ambiguity means that **you need to communicate clearly and early** with your county's building department.

Start by requesting a **pre-application meeting** with your local planning or permitting office. Come prepared with a site address, preliminary layout, and questions about specific codes. Ask what's required for:

• Structural approval (framing method, engineering stamps)

• Septic and water system design

• Driveway or easement access

• Foundation type restrictions (some counties don't allow slab-on-grade in flood zones)

• Roofing and siding material compliance

Do not assume that just because a neighbor built a barndo down the road, you can too. Zoning designations can differ from parcel to parcel—even across the same street.

You'll also need to understand the **permit flow**, which may include multiple approvals:

1 Land Use or Zoning Compliance

2 Septic or Wastewater Approval

3 Site Plan Review

4 Building Permit (often with engineered drawings required)

5 Electrical, Mechanical, and Plumbing Permits (separate in some states)

6 Final Certificate of Occupancy (C.O.)

In many rural counties, inspections are minimal and the process is flexible. In others, especially suburban fringe zones, the scrutiny can rival that of urban subdivisions. Know where your project falls on that spectrum.

Also, if you're planning to do any part of the build yourself (as an owner-builder), ask what the legal limitations are in your jurisdiction. Some states allow owner-builders to pull all their own permits; others require a licensed general contractor to oversee structural or utility work. Get that in writing before signing contracts or ordering materials.

Finally, don't rely solely on your contractor to handle this for you. Even experienced builders can overlook regional nuances—especially if they haven't worked extensively in your county. As the property owner, **you are ultimately responsible** for code compliance. Taking 2–3 hours to meet with your local code office and gather documentation can prevent 2–3 months of setbacks down the line.

Permitting is not the most glamorous part of the build. But it's where the entire project either moves forward confidently—or gets stuck before it starts. Treat it like a structural component of the build itself: foundational, necessary, and worth doing right the first time.

HOW TO DESIGN FOR REAL LIFE: LAYOUT PLANNING THAT MATCHES THE WAY YOU ACTUALLY LIVE

Designing a barndominium isn't about copying floor plans off the internet or falling in love with a trendy façade—it's about shaping a space around the way you live, work, move, and rest. And while aesthetics matter, it's function that determines whether you'll still love your home five, ten, or twenty years down the line.

I always start this conversation by asking clients one simple question: "**What frustrates you most about the space you live in now?**"

That answer almost always leads directly to a smart design decision.

For some, it's traffic flow—walking across the house to do laundry or not having direct access from the garage into the kitchen. For others, it's lack of flexibility—rooms that serve one function and sit unused half the week. In a barndominium, your layout has the freedom to break those traditional limitations, but that freedom means you must also design with **intention**.

Start by identifying your **core lifestyle zones**:

• **Work zones**: Do you need a home office, a full shop, or both?

• **Quiet zones**: Should bedrooms be grouped together or isolated for privacy?

• **Gathering zones**: Do you entertain often? Need an open kitchen/living area or prefer defined rooms?

In real builds, I've seen layouts fall apart when they were built around Pinterest inspiration instead of actual routines. A massive great room looks fantastic—until you realize the noise from the TV carries straight into the master bedroom. Likewise, putting a guest room next to the kids' bath sounds fine until you host in-laws for a week.

The key is to build **zones of activity and privacy**, especially if your home will be multi-functional. Use walls, corners, or even minor level changes to separate loud from quiet, clean from dirty, work from rest.

Another factor often missed is **flow**—how people, pets, and tools move through the space. Where do muddy boots go? Can you get from the shop to the kitchen without tracking dirt through the living room? Will you be unloading groceries from the garage, or carrying laundry across the house twice a day? These details, while small, define whether a house lives well or constantly works against you.

Storage should also be designed intentionally—not as leftover space, but as part of the plan. Walk-in pantries, mudrooms, oversized closets, attic trusses, and under-stair utility nooks are all low-cost additions that pay long-term dividends in daily use.

Finally, design for your **future, not just your present**. Leave room in the garage for expansion. Pre-frame for a second-story loft even if you don't build it yet. Rough-in plumbing where you might one day want a bathroom. The small cost of preparing now saves you thousands later when your needs evolve.

A barndominium gives you the opportunity to build something highly customized. But that customization is only valuable if it's rooted in **reality**, not guesswork. Think less about trends and more about how you want to live—and design a layout that supports it from day one.

VISUAL FLOOR PLANS WITH ANNOTATIONS: FROM COZY TO COLOSSAL

A floor plan isn't just a drawing—it's the first true translation of your lifestyle into structure. It's where the dream begins to take measurable shape. But for many new builders, this step quickly becomes overwhelming. Online templates, Pinterest galleries, and plan catalogs can lead to option fatigue without offering real context. What's often missing is not inspiration, but **interpretation**—understanding how a plan actually functions in daily life.

In this section, we're not just showcasing floor plans—we're breaking them down. You'll see a range of layouts, from compact and efficient to expansive multi-use designs. But more importantly, each example comes annotated with insights from the field: why certain layouts flow better, where storage works best, and how to anticipate daily use before the first nail is driven.

Whether you're a couple downsizing into a smaller footprint, a growing family needing separation and privacy, or a hands-on builder wanting a live-in workshop, the goal here is to give you visual clarity. Each plan reflects a different lifestyle model, and each annotation is designed to help you **translate square footage into smart function**.

Use these plans as a guide—not as a rulebook. Modify, combine, scale, and adapt them as needed. This is where you start turning concept into concrete reality.

———

🏠 **Featured Floor Plan: Compact and Efficient Starter Barndominium**

1 Bedroom | 1 Bathroom | Open-Concept Kitchen/Living Area | Front Porch

Approx. 880 sq. ft. Heated Living Space

📷 **Exterior Rendering**

This plan embraces a **modern minimalist aesthetic** while maximizing usability and affordability. The black vertical metal siding paired with light wood trim gives the home a warm, modern rural feel. Wide sliding glass doors and clean roof lines create a simple but striking profile, ideal for rural homesteads, vacation rentals, or downsized living.

• Durable, low-maintenance exterior finishes.

• Generous front porch for outdoor relaxation and entertaining.

• Compact footprint perfect for tight lots, small homesteads, or efficient off-grid builds.

◺ Floor Plan Overview

The layout prioritizes **simple flow and open living**, allowing for an oversized great room that maximizes usable space, while keeping private functions like sleeping and bathing tucked into their own efficient wing. No wasted space, no unnecessary hallways—just pure functional living.

For a quick technical summary before we dive deeper into the layout features, here are the key specifications:

▦ Quick-Glance Specs

Feature	Details
Total Heated Area	~880 sq. ft.
Bedrooms	1
Bathrooms	1 full
Laundry/Utility Area	Stackable space available
Porches	Full covered front porch
Ideal Build Style	Steel frame or post-frame
Estimated Build Cost	$85,000–$120,000 (@ $95–$135/sq.ft.)

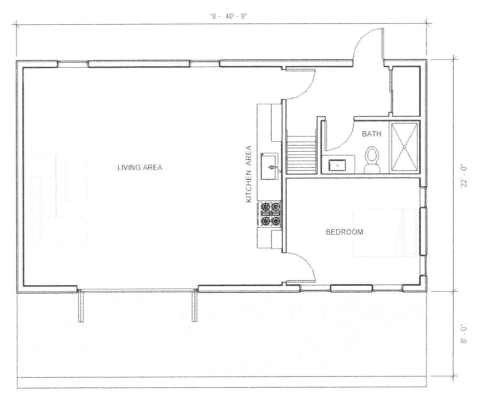

"0 - 40' - 0"

LIVING AREA

KITCHEN AREA

BATH

BEDROOM

22' - 0"

8' - 0"

❋ Plan Highlights & Layout Flow

⛃ Living Area & Kitchen (Approx. 26' × 22') – 572 sq. ft.

• Full open-concept living room seamlessly connected to the kitchen area.

• The large living area accommodates full-sized furniture, entertainment setups, and flexible seating arrangements.

• Ample space for an optional dining table or additional kitchen island/bar seating.

• Abundant natural light through the front-facing sliding glass doors.

🛏 Bedroom (Approx. 12' × 10') – 120 sq. ft.

• Cozy, functional private bedroom tucked into the back corner.

• Comfortably fits a queen-sized bed with nightstands and dresser.

• Two windows for cross-ventilation and natural lighting.

🚿 Bathroom (Approx. 6' × 8') – 48 sq. ft.

• Full bathroom with shower, vanity, and toilet.

• Smart placement adjacent to both the living area and bedroom.

• Sized to meet comfort standards without consuming excessive square footage.

▦ Entryway & Utility Area (Approx. 4' × 8') – 32 sq. ft.

• Compact transitional zone off the kitchen ideal for a stacked washer/dryer, pantry shelving, or mechanicals.

• Directly accessible from the main living space without interfering with flow.

🧠 Why This Plan Works

⚒ Designed for Practical Living:

• **Open-concept flow** maximizes the main living space, making it feel far larger than the square footage suggests.

• **Private zoning** ensures sleeping areas are shielded from entry points and public space.

• **Zero-waste floor plan**: every square foot has a purpose.

🔋 Smart, Sustainable, and Scalable:

• Small enough for **affordable solar system integration** or complete off-grid setup.

• Future expansion is possible — add a rear patio, a detached garage, or a side carport with minimal site disruption.

• Excellent investment potential as an Airbnb rental, secondary guest house, or starter property.

💡 Builder's Tips & Ideas

🔧 Construction Tip:

Pre-wire the living room ceiling for fans and future pendant lighting to enhance airflow and layered lighting options without extensive retrofits.

💰 Budget Tip:

Choose mini-split HVAC systems for cost-effective, highly efficient heating and cooling—ideal for small-volume, open-concept spaces like this one.

🔥 **Lifestyle Upgrade:**

Extend the front porch deck by an additional 4' to 6' for an outdoor dining zone without significant foundation cost increases.

🎯 **Ideal For:**

• First-time home builders seeking simple, affordable designs.

• Retirees or downsizers wanting compact, easy-to-maintain living.

• Vacation rental investors needing durable, visually appealing units.

• Off-grid homeowners or homesteaders optimizing efficiency and simplicity.

———

🏡 **Featured Floor Plan: Modern Farmhouse Barndo**

3 Bedrooms | 2 Bathrooms | Office | 2-Car Garage | Covered Front & Rear Porches

Approx. 1,800 sq. ft. | Slab or Crawlspace Foundation Option

📷 **Exterior Rendering**

This plan showcases a **black board-and-batten modern farmhouse** with warm wood post accents and a classic gabled roofline. The **front porch is fully covered**, making it ideal for rocking chairs, seasonal décor, or quiet morning coffee. Clean lines and practical trim give this home curb appeal without unnecessary complexity—making it as cost-effective as it is beautiful.

📐 **Floor Plan Overview**

The layout features a **central great room and kitchen combo**, anchored by a large island and flanked by a **split-bedroom design**—ideal for privacy and family function. A **dedicated office** at the front adds workspace versatility, and the **attached garage** connects smartly to the laundry and master suite.

For a quick technical summary before we dive deeper into the layout features, here are the key specifications:

📊 **Quick-Glance Specs**

Feature	Details
Total Area	~1,800 sq. ft.
Bedrooms	3
Bathrooms	2
Office/Flex Room	Yes
Garage	2-Car (attached)
Porches	Covered Front & Rear
Ideal Build Style	Steel frame or traditional wood
Estimated Build Cost	$180,000–$234,000 (@ $100–130/sq.ft.)

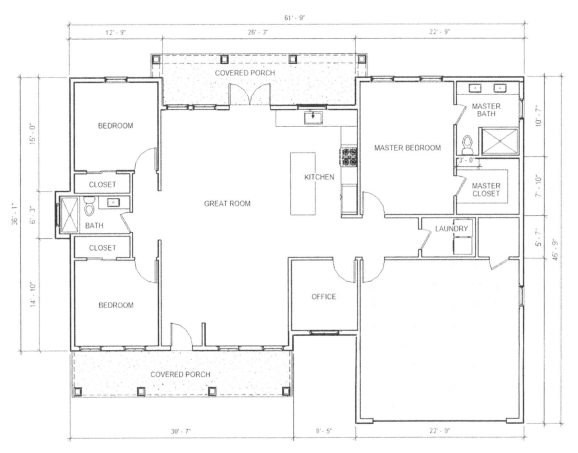

Plan Highlights & Layout Flow

Great Room & Kitchen

20

- Large open-concept space in the center of the home
- Island-style kitchen allows for seating, cooking, and socializing all in one spot
- French doors lead directly to the **covered rear porch**—great for BBQs or entertaining
- Perfect for vaulted ceilings and farmhouse light fixtures

🛏 Master Suite (Right Wing)

- Spacious master bedroom tucked away from traffic
- Large walk-in closet and full bathroom with **dual vanity** and **walk-in shower**
- Direct access to laundry room for practical daily flow

🛏 Secondary Bedrooms (Left Wing)

- Two bedrooms with closets and a **shared full bath** between
- Ideal setup for kids, guests, or in-laws
- Slight separation from the great room gives a sense of privacy

🖥 Dedicated Office

- Located at the front of the home with great natural light
- Easily convertible to a fourth bedroom, craft room, or homeschool space

🚗 Garage + Utility

- 2-car garage with interior access
- Connected to laundry for easy unload and clean-up
- Option to expand or modify for workshop or storage area

🌳 Porches (Front & Back)

- **Front porch** provides a welcoming entry and classic farmhouse feel
- **Rear porch** is full-width and covered, perfect for outdoor dining or relaxing in all weather

🧠 Why This Plan Works

🔨 Designed for Real Living:

- The **split-bedroom layout** offers privacy for the master suite, making it great for families, couples, or even multigenerational living.
- The **open great room** creates a warm, inclusive space without wasted square footage.
- A **flexible office space** means you don't have to sacrifice a bedroom to work from home.

🔋 Efficient & Affordable:

- Simple rooflines and rectangular footprint make this home **budget-friendly to build and heat**.
- Easy to insulate and adapt for **solar or off-grid upgrades**.
- Front-to-back airflow and porch shading reduce cooling needs.

💡 Builder's Tips & Ideas

🔧 Construction Tip:

Stick with a **single-slope (shed-style) roof on the porch** for quicker framing and cleaner water runoff.

💰 Budget Tip:

Use **stained concrete floors** throughout to save on flooring costs while creating a modern industrial finish that's easy to clean and lasts forever.

🔥 Lifestyle Upgrade:

Install a wood-burning stove in the great room or outdoor fireplace on the rear porch for that true barndominium lifestyle vibe.

◎ Ideal For:

• Families with children needing privacy and flexibility

• Retirees seeking single-floor living with space to host grandkids

• Remote workers needing a private home office

• DIYers or semi-DIYers building on a budget

🏠 Featured Floor Plan: Family-Friendly Barndominium with Workshop

3 Bedrooms | 2.5 Bathrooms | Open-Concept Great Room | Laundry Room | Attached Garage/Workshop | Covered Front Porch

Approx. 2,400–2,500 sq. ft. Heated Living Space + Workshop

📷 Exterior Rendering

This plan combines **classic rustic appeal** with **modern functionality**. The **timber-framed entry gable** paired with vertical siding and metal roofing delivers striking curb appeal while emphasizing durability and low maintenance.

Large, divided-light windows flood the interior with natural light, making it feel welcoming and expansive.

• Full-length **covered front porch** for true country living vibes.

• Durable exterior materials built for rural, suburban, or even semi-urban lots.

• The balance of symmetrical wings and central entry provides timeless architectural appeal.

📐 Floor Plan Overview

This design offers **a true family living layout**: a large, central great room and kitchen at the heart of the home, with private bedroom wings.

The **oversized attached garage/workshop** adds serious function, making it ideal for tradespeople, hobbyists, or those needing flexible work-from-home space.

For a quick technical summary before we dive deeper into the layout features, here are the key specifications:

📊 Quick-Glance Specs

Feature	Details
Total Heated Area	~2,400–2,500 sq. ft.
Garage/Workshop Area	~1,100 sq. ft.
Bedrooms	3
Bathrooms	2.5 (2 full + 1 half)
Laundry Room	Dedicated with extra storage
Porches	Full covered front porch
Ideal Build Style	Steel frame or heavy post-frame
Estimated Build Cost	$260,000–$340,000 (@ $105–$130/sq.ft.)

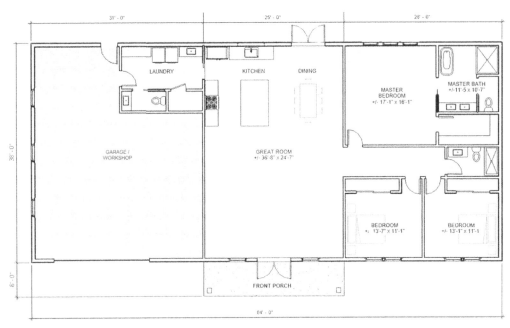

⊛ **Plan Highlights & Layout Flow**

🏠 **Great Room, Kitchen, and Dining (Approx. 36'5" × 24'7") – ~900 sq. ft.**

- Massive open-concept space perfect for large gatherings and family living.

- Centrally located kitchen with large island offering workspace and casual dining.

- Rear French doors extend entertainment possibilities onto future patios or porches.

- Dining area adjacent to kitchen allows for formal or casual mealtime flexibility.

🛏 **Master Suite (Approx. 17'7" × 16'1" bedroom + 11'5" × 10'7" bath)**

- Spacious master bedroom suite located on its own private wing.

- Includes a luxurious en-suite master bath with walk-in shower, double vanities, and ample linen storage.

- Room for a private seating area or additional built-ins.

🛏 **Secondary Bedrooms (Each Approx. 13'7" × 11'1")**

- Two identical secondary bedrooms perfect for kids, guests, or dual offices.

- Shared full bathroom centrally located between the two rooms.

- Layout creates a semi-private "children's wing" separated from the master suite.

🧹 **Laundry & Half Bath Area**

- Smartly placed laundry room directly accessible from the kitchen and garage.

- Additional half-bath (powder room) for guests and quick-access needs.

- Mechanical/storage space hidden but easily reachable for future maintenance.

🚗 **Garage/Workshop (Approx. 31' × 36') – ~1,100 sq. ft.**

- Oversized garage accommodates two to three vehicles with additional workshop space.

- Large enough for workbenches, woodworking, vehicle maintenance, or a home-based business.

- High side walls offer potential for loft storage, studio space, or expansion.

🧠 **Why This Plan Works**

🔨 **Designed for Functional Family Living:**

- Central great room ensures family togetherness without sacrificing personal privacy.

- Master suite separation ensures a peaceful retreat even with a busy household.

- Oversized garage/workshop adds massive versatility for professional or hobbyist use.

🔋 **Efficient and Expandable:**

- Smart rectangular footprint simplifies framing and HVAC routing, improving energy efficiency.

- Open wall space along the great room can accommodate future expansions like sunrooms or rear decks.

- Ample space for solar installations or water catchment systems if building off-grid.

💡 **Builder's Tips & Ideas**

🔧 **Construction Tip:**

Frame extra-deep garage walls (2x8 construction) for better insulation and sound buffering between living and work areas.

⬧ Budget Tip:

Stub out plumbing into the garage during the slab pour—future-proof the shop for a full bathroom, wet bar, or apartment conversion.

⬧ Lifestyle Upgrade:

Pre-wire for outdoor speakers and lighting on the front porch—small cost upfront, huge boost to outdoor living quality.

⬧ Ideal For:

• Growing families needing separation between adult and kid spaces.

• Tradespeople or entrepreneurs wanting to work from home.

• Homesteaders or rural dwellers needing storage, shop, and living space in one package.

• Buyers who prioritize flexibility and future adaptability.

———

⬧ Featured Floor Plan: Compact Work-and-Live Barndominium with Oversized Workshop

2 Bedrooms | 1 Bathroom | Open-Concept Kitchen and Great Room | Laundry Nook | Attached Garage/Workshop | Rear and Entry Porches

Approx. 1,000–1,100 sq. ft. Heated Living Space + Workshop

⬧ Exterior Rendering

This design delivers **modern functionality** with **classic country aesthetics**. Vertical board-and-batten siding paired with a high-pitched metal roof and exposed trusses over the entry gives the home a welcoming, durable look perfect for a wide range of rural and suburban lots.

• Full glass doors connect indoor living to outdoor spaces easily.

• Compact, symmetrical design optimized for fast, affordable construction.

• Inviting **entry porch** and **rear grilling porch** maximize usability without blowing the budget.

⬧ Floor Plan Overview

Designed for efficiency and practicality, this layout offers **true multipurpose living**:

Compact but comfortable private living quarters, attached to a **huge garage/workshop** for business, hobbies, or flexible storage.

Ideal for tradespeople, small families, retirees, or anyone needing space for both living and working.

For a quick technical summary before we dive deeper into the layout features, here are the key specifications:

⬧ Quick-Glance Specs

Feature	Details
Total Heated Area	~1,000–1,100 sq. ft.
Garage/Workshop Area	~1,600 sq. ft.
Bedrooms	2
Bathrooms	1 full + 1 half (in shop)
Laundry Nook	Yes (stackable or closet setup)
Porches	Covered front entry + rear grilling porch
Ideal Build Style	Steel frame or post-frame
Estimated Build Cost	$190,000–$250,000 (@ $95–$115/sq.ft. main + shop cost adjustments)

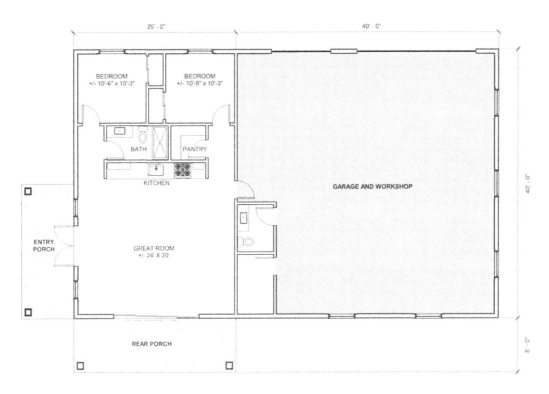

25' - 0"

40' - 0"

BEDROOM
+/- 10'-6" x 10'-3"

BEDROOM
+/- 10'-6" x 10'-3"

BATH

PANTRY

KITCHEN

GARAGE AND WORKSHOP

40' - 0"

ENTRY
PORCH

GREAT ROOM
+/- 24' X 20'

REAR PORCH

8' - 0"

✸ Plan Highlights & Layout Flow

🏛 Great Room and Kitchen (Approx. 24' × 20') – 480 sq. ft.

• Spacious, open-concept area serving as the core living and social hub.

• Kitchen flows directly into the living space, with room for a dining table or island.

• Direct access to rear grilling porch extends usable living space for outdoor dining or relaxation.

🛏 Bedrooms (Each Approx. 10'6" × 10'3") – ~108 sq. ft. per bedroom

• Two well-proportioned bedrooms with standard closets.

• Perfect setup for two family members, guest accommodation, or a home office.

• Efficient placement adjacent to the shared bathroom for smooth daily routines.

🚿 Bathroom

• Full bath located centrally between both bedrooms.

• Includes shower, vanity, and efficient fixture placement for space savings.

🚗 Garage and Workshop (Approx. 40' × 40') – 1,600 sq. ft.

• Massive attached garage dominates the floor plan, making this design ideal for home businesses, heavy storage needs, or mechanical hobbies.

• Enough room for vehicle lifts, woodworking equipment, or large-scale projects.

• Includes a secondary half-bath easily accessible from the shop side—keeps work grime out of the main living space.

🧹 Additional Features

• Pantry closet adjacent to kitchen for storage efficiency.

• Mechanical room located in the shop area for easy access and maintenance without disrupting living spaces.

• Entry porch provides a covered, weather-protected entrance directly into the great room.

✸ Why This Plan Works

🔨 Designed for Work-Life Integration:

• True live-and-work design with clear separation of private and business spaces.

• Oversized garage/shop offers incredible flexibility for professional trades or serious hobbyists.

• Great room and kitchen flow allows a small family to live comfortably without feeling cramped.

🗄 Smart, Scalable, and Efficient:

• High shop ceilings (possible) allow for future mezzanine or storage loft installations.

• Tight, simple footprint keeps construction costs and timelines under control.

• Expandability options available: convert shop space into future additional bedrooms, office suites, or apartments if needed.

💡 Builder's Tips & Ideas

🔧 Construction Tip:

Consider framing 12' or 14' sidewalls in the garage section to allow installation of automotive lifts or mezzanine storage decks later.

💰 Budget Tip:

Finish the living space fully first, then rough-finish the shop area if needed to control immediate costs—easy to complete the shop in phases.

🔥 Lifestyle Upgrade:

Pre-run conduit for high-amp service in the garage/shop (220V or 240V outlets)—future-proofs the building for welding equipment, heavy tools, or RV charging.

◎ Ideal For:

• Tradespeople, mechanics, or contractors needing on-site workspaces.

• Retirees or rural families wanting a minimalistic home paired with serious shop space.

• Buyers focused on **livable simplicity with practical work capacity**.

• Off-grid builders needing flexible layouts for solar, water collection, and workshop utilities.

———

🏡 Featured Floor Plan: Expanded Family Barndominium with Office and Outdoor Patio

3 Bedrooms | 2 Bathrooms | Dedicated Office | Open-Concept Kitchen and Great Room | Laundry Room | Outdoor Living Patio | Covered Front Porch

Approx. 2,200–2,300 sq. ft. Heated Living Space

📸 Exterior Rendering

This design blends **modern farmhouse appeal** with **classic symmetry**. Vertical board-and-batten siding in a rich dark tone gives the home a sleek, durable finish while **natural wood porch columns** add warmth and character.

• **Full covered front porch** with centered entryway for a commanding, balanced facade.

• Twin gables add vertical dimension and elegance without complicating the roofline.

• Lush landscaping options pair naturally with this straightforward structure.

📐 Floor Plan Overview

This home is designed for **modern family living**, offering a **clear division between private and social spaces**.

It features a **split-bedroom layout** for maximum privacy, a dedicated **home office**, and a stunning **outdoor patio** directly accessible from the great room and kitchen.

The layout prioritizes open flow, efficiency, and future adaptability—all anchored around a **central communal core**.

For a quick technical summary before we dive deeper into the layout features, here are the key specifications:

🔢 Quick-Glance Specs

Feature	Details
Total Heated Area	~2,200–2,300 sq. ft.
Bedrooms	3
Bathrooms	2 full
Office	1 dedicated (convertible space)
Outdoor Patio	Yes (~396 sq. ft.)
Laundry Room	Full size with exterior access
Porches	Full front porch + rear outdoor patio
Ideal Build Style	Steel frame or heavy post-frame
Estimated Build Cost	$270,000–$350,000 (@ $115–$135/sq.ft.)

⊛ **Plan Highlights & Layout Flow**

🛋️ **Great Room and Kitchen (Approx. 43' × 20') – ~860 sq. ft.**

• Massive open-concept great room ideal for large family gatherings or entertaining.

• Oversized kitchen island perfect for casual dining, meal prep, and socializing.

• Direct sightlines from the kitchen through to the outdoor patio space.

• Full wall of windows and rear access doors enhance natural light and connection to outdoor living.

🛏️ **Master Suite (Bedroom: Approx. 16' × 12'11", Bath: 9' × 12'11")**

• Private master wing completely separated from other bedrooms.

• Spacious master bedroom with direct access to the luxury master bath.

• Master bathroom includes a walk-in shower, dual vanities, private toilet area, and connection to a full walk-in closet.

🛏️ **Secondary Bedrooms (Each Approx. 14'5" × 12'2" and 14'5" × 8'7")**

• Two well-sized secondary bedrooms on the opposite side of the house from the master.

• Ideal for families with children, guests, or even flexible use (hobby rooms, dual offices, etc.).

• Shared access to a full bathroom positioned centrally between the rooms.

💻 **Home Office (Approx. 10'7" × 8'7")**

• Dedicated office at the front of the home—quiet, private, and practical.

• Positioned perfectly for remote workers, homeschool needs, or flex-use as a small guest room.

🚿 **Bathrooms**

• Master Bath: Full suite with luxury features.

• Secondary Bath: Efficiently designed with full tub/shower combo, double sinks, and adjacent to the secondary bedrooms.

🧹 **Laundry and Utility Room**

• Full laundry room connected to the rear patio and near the secondary bedrooms for easy daily access.

• Smart placement makes utility tasks streamlined without interfering with the home's main flow.

🌳 **Outdoor Living**

• Central **outdoor patio** (~18' × 22') seamlessly extends indoor living space outdoors.

• Perfect for a future pergola, outdoor kitchen, or even a screened-in patio upgrade.

🧠 **Why This Plan Works**

🔨 **Designed for Family, Work, and Play:**

• Split-bedroom plan ensures privacy for adults and children alike.

• Office placement offers true separation for remote working needs.

• Outdoor patio designed to flow naturally off main living spaces—perfect for year-round usability.

📱 **Efficient, Elegant, and Expandable:**

• Smart rectangular footprint reduces HVAC and foundation costs.

• Ample wall space for solar panel integration.

• Clear potential to expand living areas toward the rear or sides without disrupting core systems.

💡 Builder's Tips & Ideas

🔧 Construction Tip:

Use oversized patio doors or sliding walls to maximize indoor-outdoor connectivity for entertaining.

💰 Budget Tip:

If budget requires, rough-in utilities for the outdoor patio kitchen now—even if you finish it later.

🔥 Lifestyle Upgrade:

Install retractable awnings or pergola systems over the patio area to dramatically extend seasonal use without a full hard cover.

🎯 Ideal For:

• Families needing functional separation between kids' rooms and master suite.

• Remote workers or entrepreneurs wanting dedicated, distraction-free office space.

• Homeowners prioritizing outdoor living without major expansion costs.

• Buyers seeking a **balanced, adaptable** home with premium flow and curb appeal.

———

🏡 Featured Floor Plan: Modern Rustic Barndominium with Garage and Workshop

3 Bedrooms | 2 Bathrooms | Open-Concept Kitchen and Great Room | Dedicated Laundry Area | Garage/Workshop | Front Covered Porch

Approx. 1,700–1,800 sq. ft. Heated Living Space + Garage

📷 Exterior Rendering

This barndominium showcases a **warm, rustic look** with **modern structural efficiency**. Natural wood siding, a **timber-framed front gable**, and **stone foundation details** create a beautiful, timeless exterior, perfect for rural, suburban, or wooded lots.

• Large **covered front porch** expands living space and enhances curb appeal.

• High-pitch standing seam metal roof for durability and weather resistance.

• Symmetrical design balances charm and structural practicality.

📐 Floor Plan Overview

This layout is tailored for **family-focused living**, combining spacious indoor gathering areas with quiet private bedrooms.

The **attached garage and workshop** provides a seamless transition from work to home life, with mechanical access smartly separated from the living quarters.

For a quick technical summary before we dive deeper into the layout features, here are the key specifications:

📊 Quick-Glance Specs

Feature	Details
Total Heated Area	~1,700–1,800 sq. ft.
Garage/Workshop Area	~710 sq. ft.
Bedrooms	3
Bathrooms	2 full
Laundry Room	Yes (separate, not in garage)
Porches	Full covered front porch
Ideal Build Style	Post-frame or hybrid steel frame
Estimated Build Cost	$220,000–$290,000 (@ $110–$130/sq.ft.)

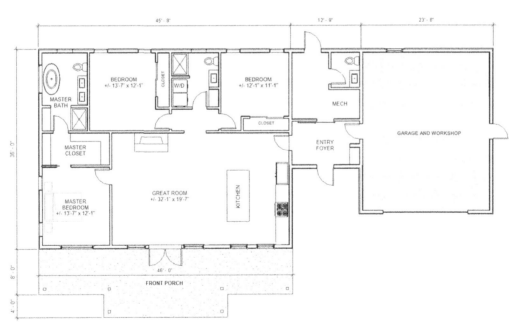

⊕ **Plan Highlights & Layout Flow**

🏛 **Great Room and Kitchen (Approx. 32'1" × 19'7") – ~630 sq. ft.**

- Expansive great room anchored by the front door entry, centered around a large open-concept space.

- Generous kitchen island creates a hub for cooking, entertaining, and casual meals.

- Flow directly connects kitchen, dining, and living areas without barriers.

🛏 **Master Suite (Bedroom: Approx. 15'3" × 12'1", Bath: generously sized)**

- Spacious master bedroom tucked away for privacy on one side of the house.

- Features a luxurious master bath with soaking tub, shower, and dual vanities.

- Full walk-in master closet located between the bedroom and bathroom for seamless dressing flow.

🛏 **Secondary Bedrooms**

- **Bedroom 2 (Approx. 15'3" × 12'1")** — large enough for queen bed setups, ideal for teenagers or guests.

- **Bedroom 3 (Approx. 12'4" × 11'1")** — slightly smaller but still comfortably fits a full/queen bed.

- Secondary bedrooms share a full bath, located conveniently off the hallway near the laundry area.

🚿 **Bathrooms**

- Master Bath: Spa-like experience with oversized tub, walk-in shower, and double vanity.

- Shared Secondary Bath: Full-service bathroom with standard tub/shower combo.

🧹 **Laundry and Mechanical Room**

- Dedicated laundry space between secondary bedrooms—easy access for family functionality.

- Mechanical room near the garage entry, keeping systems accessible but hidden from living spaces.

🚗 **Garage and Workshop (Approx. 23'8" × 30') – ~710 sq. ft.**

- Attached garage/workshop is large enough for two vehicles plus workshop or storage space.

- Positioned to allow easy home access without disrupting the main living zones.

- Could be used for professional trades, hobbies, or additional home storage.

🧠 **Why This Plan Works**

🔨 **Designed for Practical Daily Living:**

- Split-bedroom layout protects privacy and separates sleeping from social spaces.

- Direct but discreet access between garage and home for functionality without disrupting flow.

- Great room offers oversized flexibility for family gatherings, movie nights, or large-scale entertaining.

📱 **Smart, Flexible, and Ready to Grow:**

- Rear site allows easy future expansion: outdoor patios, decks, or even detached guest houses.

- Garage prepped for future shop buildouts, tool spaces, or equipment storage.

- Clear access points for solar arrays or rainwater catchment systems if desired.

💡 **Builder's Tips & Ideas**

🔧 **Construction Tip:**

Upgrade the front porch foundation with stone piers or concrete footers for longevity—small investment, major visual and structural gain.

ᔍ Budget Tip:

Pre-frame loft trusses above the garage if you foresee needing bonus storage or a future bonus room—cost-effective to do during original framing.

ᗡ Lifestyle Upgrade:

Rough-in water and electrical in the garage—adds serious resale value if you later build out a full workshop, home gym, or secondary suite.

◎ Ideal For:

• Families with children seeking smart zoning between parents and kids.

• Hobbyists or small-business owners needing integrated work/living spaces.

• Rural buyers wanting a visually striking home with real long-term flexibility.

• Homeowners balancing practicality with classic rustic-modern charm.

This floor plan brings **a traditional family barndominium layout with refined details**—perfect for readers serious about balancing **beauty, daily functionality, and future-proof design**.

———

⌂ Featured Floor Plan: Modern Rustic Barndominium with Workshop

3 Bedrooms | 2 Bathrooms | Laundry/Mudroom | Attached Garage/Workshop | Covered Front & Rear Porches

Approx. 2,100–2,200 sq. ft. of Heated Living Space | Plus Workshop Area

▣ Exterior Rendering

This design blends **industrial modern** with **classic farmhouse charm**. A **bold black metal exterior** is paired with **natural wood accents** under a traditional gabled roofline. The result is a commanding presence that's both functional and stylish.

• Massive **floor-to-ceiling windows** in the shop area flood the workspace with natural light.

• The **full-length front porch** and **extended rear grilling porch** create true indoor-outdoor living potential.

• Perfect for those who want a working property that still feels warm and livable.

◲ Floor Plan Overview

The layout smartly separates **living areas from workspaces**, offering privacy and sound control without sacrificing flow. The **central great room** connects the heart of the home, while the master suite is strategically isolated for peace and quiet.

For a quick technical summary before we dive deeper into the layout features, here are the key specifications:

Quick-Glance Specs

Feature	Details
Total Heated Area	~2,100–2,200 sq. ft.
Garage/Workshop	~700 sq. ft. additional
Bedrooms	3
Bathrooms	2 full
Laundry/Mudroom	Yes (connected to Master Closet)
Porches	Full front + Extended rear
Ideal Build Style	Steel frame or heavy post-frame
Estimated Build Cost	$210,000–$280,000 (@ $95–125/sq.ft.)

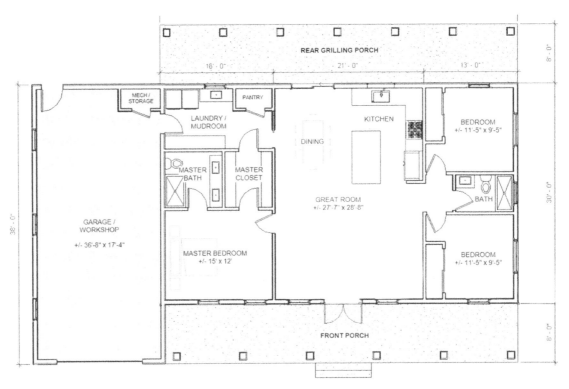

⚜ **Plan Highlights & Layout Flow**

🏠 Great Room, Kitchen & Dining

• Centralized **great room** sized generously at nearly 28' x 28'

• Massive open concept blending kitchen, living, and dining for effortless hosting and family living

• Oversized kitchen island ideal for seating, prep, and casual meals

• Dining area flows directly into rear porch for **seamless grilling and entertaining**

🛏 Master Suite (Left Wing)

• Located on the opposite side of the secondary bedrooms for maximum privacy

• Includes **walk-in closet** and **private master bath** with dedicated shower area

• Direct access to the **laundry/mudroom** from the master closet—designed for real-world efficiency

🛏 Secondary Bedrooms (Right Wing)

• Two secondary bedrooms, each with standard closets

• Shared full bathroom conveniently located between bedrooms

• Ideal for children, guests, or home offices

🚪 Laundry/Mudroom + Pantry

• Functional drop zone between the garage and main living space

• Provides essential daily flow: clean-up, gear storage, and pantry organization

• Mudroom design helps keep dirt out of main living areas—critical for rural builds

🚗 Garage/Workshop

• Huge **36'8" x 17'4"** space—enough for two vehicles plus a substantial workshop area

• Mechanicals and storage tucked smartly into a corner

• Floor-to-ceiling glass wall in the workshop area provides natural lighting for projects

• Garage is attached yet acoustically separated from the main home

🌳 Outdoor Spaces

• **Covered front porch** for classic country curb appeal

• **Massive rear grilling porch** that extends living space outside—perfect for BBQs, outdoor kitchens, or even a future screened-in porch

🧠 Why This Plan Works

⚒ Designed for Practical Living:

• Work and living spaces are logically separated, but easily accessed

• Centralized gathering space maximizes usable square footage without wasted hallways

• Rear grilling porch enhances the home's entertainment capacity

🔋 Efficient, Flexible, and Future-Proof:

• Workshop space could later be converted to an apartment, rental unit, or expanded living area

• Smart flow reduces HVAC loads, especially with a south or east rear orientation

• Allows for phased expansion—future owners could build onto either side without disturbing core structure

💡 **Builder's Tips & Ideas**

🔧 **Construction Tip:**

Frame in extra heavy-duty headers above garage doors during initial build. If you ever upgrade to larger equipment or RV storage, you'll thank yourself later.

💰 **Budget Tip:**

Install rough plumbing in the workshop during slab pour. Even if unused now, it gives the option to add a half-bath or kitchenette later without major demolition.

🔥 **Lifestyle Upgrade:**

Screen-in the rear porch or add roll-down shades to maximize its use across multiple seasons, particularly in hotter or buggy climates.

🎯 **Ideal For:**

• Entrepreneurs or tradespeople needing dedicated workspace at home

• Growing families seeking functional, open living space

• Hobbyists, woodworkers, mechanics, or RV owners

• Buyers prioritizing flexibility, resale value, and outdoor living options

———

Ready to see real possibilities for your dream barndominium?

Get instant access to a curated pack of **full-color, annotated floor plans** — designed to inspire your layout, optimize your space, and avoid common mistakes.

Print them, sketch on them, or bring them to your builder.

Bring your dream one step closer. Scan and Download your Floor Plan Inspiration Pack now.

CUSTOMIZING YOUR LAYOUT: TOOLS, SPACE-PLANNING HACKS, AND MULTIPURPOSE DESIGN

Designing a barndominium isn't about copying a floor plan off the internet — it's about **tailoring a living space to fit the way you want to live today — and tomorrow.**

Customization is where your project transforms from a simple structure into a truly personal home.

In this section, we'll focus on practical strategies, proven tools, and real-world techniques that help you think like a builder and a designer at the same time — so you can maximize every inch of your barndo's potential without adding unnecessary costs or regrets.

1. Layout Tools You Should Actually Use (Not Overwhelm Yourself)

Professional builders and architects rely on a few simple but powerful tools to sketch, measure, and adjust floor plans without drowning in overcomplicated software.

Here are the **tools I recommend** for practical, real-world barndominium planning:

• **Graph Paper and a Mechanical Pencil:**

It may sound basic, but nothing beats sketching rough ideas to scale on 1/4" graph paper when you're brainstorming layouts.

• **Room Sketcher / HomeByMe (Free Versions):**

These beginner-friendly online tools allow you to drag-and-drop walls, doors, windows, and furniture to visualize your layout quickly without needing architectural degrees.

• **Laser Distance Measurer:**

Essential if you're modifying existing spaces or fitting pre-engineered kits. These tools quickly help you measure and plan door swings, appliance gaps, and furniture layouts.

• **Printable Cutouts for Furniture and Fixtures:**

Some builders print scale models of beds, sofas, kitchen islands, etc., and move them around scaled drawings like puzzle pieces.

Simple? Yes. Effective? Extremely.

Pro Tip:

Don't waste six months learning AutoCAD or Revit if you're not a professional draftsman. For 90% of custom barndominiums, basic scaled drawings and simple drag-and-drop apps are more than enough.

2. Space-Planning Hacks That Maximize Every Inch

Good floor plans feel effortless — but behind that effortlessness are dozens of tiny decisions that save space and create better daily flow.

Here are **practical hacks** used by professional designers that you can apply to your own barndo:

• **Shrink Hallways:**

Hallways are dead square footage. Combine passageways into living spaces where possible. Aim for **3'–4' wide paths** integrated into open-concept designs rather than separate corridors.

• **Think Diagonally:**

Angling kitchen islands or entryways can trick the eye into perceiving more space, especially in narrow homes.

• **Use the "Five-Foot Rule":**

Any heavily used zone (kitchen, bath, laundry) should have **at least 5 feet** of clearance for moving around without bumping into obstacles — otherwise the home will feel cramped.

• **Line-of-Sight Expansion:**

Design long, clear sightlines from the entry to windows, patios, or exterior doors. It mentally expands small interiors and makes open-concept spaces feel grander.

• **Pocket Doors and Barn Doors:**

Swing doors eat up 10–15 square feet per door. Using pocket doors in tight areas (bathrooms, laundry, pantries) instantly recovers usable space without feeling "cheap."

• **Merge Functions:**

Combine mudroom, laundry, and storage into one transitional space to save square footage and simplify plumbing.

3. Multipurpose Spaces That Future-Proof Your Home

The smartest barndominiums don't just serve one phase of life — they **adapt** as families grow, careers shift, or lifestyles change.

Here are **future-proof multipurpose ideas** you should integrate early:

• **Home Office or Guest Room Combo:**

Design one bedroom with dual-purpose built-ins (like a fold-down Murphy bed or wall desk). Today's office can become tomorrow's guest suite effortlessly.

• **Garage-to-Living Space Potential:**

Plan garage ceilings tall enough and stub-in plumbing/electrical during initial construction. Later, if needed, the garage can easily become an apartment, game room, or rental suite.

• **Flex Spaces Off the Great Room:**

A "bonus room" doesn't have to be wasted. Small nooks or flexible sitting areas adjacent to living rooms can transform into kids' playrooms, music rooms, homeschool hubs, or secondary lounges.

• **Outdoor Living Zones:**

Design rear patios, grilling porches, and decks to accommodate future enclosures. Screen them later or build sunrooms without reworking foundation or rooflines.

• **Expandable Storage Areas:**

Unfinished attic trusses above garages or porches provide inexpensive future square footage for seasonal storage, craft rooms, or private studios.

Closing Thought: Plan for Today, Prepare for Tomorrow

Customization isn't just about having granite counters or trendy fixtures. It's about shaping your barndominium into a tool that fits your **real lifestyle**, grows with your family, and **avoids costly mistakes later**.

If you think through **flow, flexibility, and future use** now, you'll build a home that doesn't just work today — it keeps working for decades to come.

BUDGET PLANNING TOOLS AND TIMELINES (WITH A DOWNLOADABLE WORKSHEET)

When it comes to building your barndominium, **money mistakes** are the fastest way to turn a dream into a disaster.

Overbudgeting can delay your project. Underbudgeting can kill it altogether.

Here's the truth:

Even if you hire the best contractors, the ultimate responsibility for keeping your build on track — financially and timewise — falls on **you**.

In this section, we'll break down the **real tools** and **practical methods** you need to **budget smartly and plan timelines** realistically — before the first shovel hits dirt.

1. The Right Budgeting Tools (Not Overcomplicated Software)

Forget endless spreadsheets unless you love them. For most barndominium builders, **simple, structured tools** work better.

Here's what works best in the field:

• **Simple Budget Template (Worksheet):**

A well-organized Excel sheet or printable PDF where you can track expected costs vs. actual costs across key categories (site prep, foundation, framing, utilities, finishes, contingency).

• **Cost Estimation Apps (Optional):**

Tools like BuildBook or CoConstruct help you predict rough costs, but they work best if you already have quotes in hand.

• **Local Contractor Estimates:**

Before locking your budget, **always request multiple estimates** for major categories:

○ Site prep and utilities

○ Slab and foundation

○ Framing materials and labor

○ Roofing and siding

○ Electrical, plumbing, HVAC systems

⚡ **Pro Tip:**

Request "labor only" and "material + labor" bids separately when possible. This helps you spot where DIY or material sourcing could save you big money.

2. How to Build a Realistic Barndominium Budget

Category	Typical % of Total Cost
Land Purchase + Prep	15–20%
Foundation/Slab	10–15%
Structural Shell (Framing + Roof)	25–30%
Interior Build-Out (Finishes)	25–30%
Systems (Plumbing, Electrical, HVAC)	10–15%
Permits, Fees, Inspections	2–5%
Contingency Reserve	10% minimum

Too often, new builders only focus on construction costs. But a real-world budget must cover **everything** including:

Important:

If you are managing your build yourself (acting as owner-builder), you must also budget for **project insurance**, **temporary utilities**, and **tool/equipment rental**.

3. Timeline Planning: How Long It Really Takes

Building a barndominium usually follows these **major timeline phases**:

Phase	Typical Duration
Land Acquisition + Financing	1–2 months
Design + Permits	2–4 months
Site Preparation + Foundation	1–2 months
Shell Erection (Framing & Roofing)	1–2 months
Rough-ins (Plumbing, Electric, HVAC)	1–2 months
Interior Finishes	2–4 months
Final Inspections + Punchlist	1 month

Realistic Total Timeline:

☑ Owner-Builder: **10–14 months**

☑ Contractor-Built: **8–12 months**

📋 **Downloadable Worksheet: Budget and Timeline Tracker**

To make life easier, I've created a simple **Downloadable Budget and Timeline Worksheet** that you can print or fill digitally.

It's designed for **real people**, not just professional project managers.

Use this worksheet religiously. Update it every time you get a new bid, place a material order, or adjust a schedule.

🧠 **Closing Thought: Budget for Reality, Build for Success**

Planning your money and your time with **discipline and visibility** doesn't kill your dream — it protects it.

The happiest barndominium owners aren't the ones who spent the most.

They're the ones who **stayed in control** from Day One.

If you master your budget and timeline early, you won't just build a house — you'll build freedom.

CHAPTER 3
BUILD SMART, SPEND LESS

Your Step-by-Step Construction Guide to Avoid Costly Mistakes and Build With Confidence

Building a barndominium isn't just about nailing boards and pouring concrete. It's about **making the right decision at every stage**—so your project stays on time, on budget, and becomes the home you envisioned from day one.

In construction, mistakes aren't just frustrating; they're expensive.

Every wrong material order, overlooked inspection, or miscommunication with a contractor can set you back weeks — and cost thousands.

In this chapter, you'll find a **clear, step-by-step breakdown** of the construction process, not just from a theoretical perspective, but **from the trenches**: practical advice from real builds.

We'll show you how to stay in control even when the unexpected happens — because it always does.

From **breaking ground** to **final walk-through**, you'll learn how to anticipate problems before they happen, how to communicate effectively with your crew, and how to make informed calls when changes are needed.

You'll also see where **budget traps** typically hide — and how smart planning, honest assessments, and a few professional tricks can keep you from falling into them.

Whether you're hiring it out or managing the build yourself, this chapter is your roadmap to **building smart, saving money, and building it right the first time**.

MATERIALS THAT LAST — AND THOSE THAT COST MORE THAN THEY'RE WORTH

One of the biggest advantages of building a barndominium is **control over your materials**.

Unlike buying a production home, you can choose exactly where to invest — and where to hold back.

But smart material selection isn't just about chasing durability or slashing costs.

It's about knowing **where durability matters most**, and **where "luxury upgrades" just drain your budget without adding real value**.

In this section, you'll learn how to **prioritize materials like a builder**, not a showroom shopper—so your home stands strong for decades without breaking your budget before the walls even go up.

Materials Worth Every Penny

Roofing:

Invest in standing seam metal roofing if your budget allows.

• Lifespan: 40–70+ years

• Extremely resistant to wind, hail, and fire.

• Lower maintenance and lower insurance premiums in many regions.

• Traditional shingle roofs may be cheaper up front but often require replacement in 15–20 years.

Bottom line: Metal roofing = lower long-term cost.

Framing and Structure:

Post-frame or steel framing systems are the foundation of barndominium success.

• Steel structures resist rot, termites, and warping.

• Post-frame structures are faster and cheaper to erect with wide open spans (ideal for open-concept living).

Bottom line: Never cheap out on your building skeleton. It's the one place cutting corners costs you the most later.

Insulation:

Closed-cell spray foam insulation delivers the best return for energy savings.

• Higher R-value per inch compared to fiberglass batts.

• Provides an air seal, reducing heating/cooling loads dramatically.

• Adds minor structural strength to walls and roofs.

Bottom line: Spend more on insulation once—save on heating/cooling forever.

Siding:

Metal siding panels (with proper coatings) resist weather, pests, and fire better than vinyl or wood.

• Requires little maintenance compared to wood or composite alternatives.

• Easily color-customizable with baked-on finishes.

Bottom line: It's not just about looks — it's about keeping your maintenance costs low for life.

Materials That Drain Your Budget (Without Giving Real Value)

High-End Flooring (in High-Wear Zones):

• Imported hardwoods, specialty tiles, or trendy floors are attractive but not cost-effective in workshops, mudrooms, or high-traffic areas.

• Consider luxury vinyl plank (LVP) or sealed concrete — tough, waterproof, easy to replace if needed.

Bottom line: Save fancy floors for main living areas if your budget is tight.

Custom Cabinets (Early Stage):

• It's tempting to splurge on custom cabinetry during the build. But unless cabinetry is a core feature of your home's identity, it's better to install high-quality semi-custom units and upgrade later.

Bottom line: Modular systems or unfinished cabinets let you finish beautifully without budget shock.

Premium Countertops Everywhere:

• Solid-surface countertops (quartz, granite) are fantastic for kitchens, but unnecessary for secondary bathrooms, laundry rooms, or workshops.

• Laminate surfaces today are far more attractive and durable than their reputation suggests — and cost half as much.

Bottom line: Focus your upgrades where they'll be seen and used most.

Over-the-Top Smart Home Systems:

• Full home automation (lights, HVAC, appliances) sounds great until you're troubleshooting internet outages or paying double for minor features you'll rarely use.

• Prioritize smart thermostats or energy-efficient devices first, and leave full automation for later upgrades if needed.

Bottom line: Build your home to work when Wi-Fi doesn't.

🧠 Closing Thought: Build the Skeleton First, Dress It Up Later

When you plan your material budget smartly, you give yourself the flexibility to **live well now** and **upgrade beautifully over time**.

Prioritize structure, durability, and energy performance first.

Cosmetic upgrades can always come later — but structural regrets are forever.

A well-built barndominium isn't a showroom — it's a **hardworking, efficient, beautiful reflection of your life**.

Build it that way from the inside out.

BUDGETING YOUR BUILD: REALISTIC EXAMPLES AND CONTRACTOR RED FLAGS

One of the hardest truths in building a barndominium is this:

You can have the best floor plan in the world — and still blow your entire project if you mismanage your budget or trust the wrong contractor.

In this section, we'll walk through **realistic budgeting examples**, and I'll show you **red flags** professional builders spot immediately when reviewing bids or hiring contractors.

Smart money decisions don't just happen at the start — they happen **at every phase** of the build.

📊 Realistic Budget Example: A Mid-Size Barndominium Build

Let's assume you are building a **2,400 sq. ft.** barndominium, with a modest 1,000 sq. ft. attached garage.

☑ Moderate finish levels (nice, but not luxury)

☑ Slab foundation

☑ Basic landscaping included

Estimated Build Breakdown:

Category	Typical Cost Range
Land Prep & Utilities	$25,000–$40,000
Foundation (Concrete Slab)	$20,000–$28,000
Structural Shell (Framing, Roof, Siding)	$80,000–$110,000
Interior Build-Out (Drywall, Flooring, Cabinets)	$70,000–$100,000
Plumbing/Electrical/HVAC	$40,000–$55,000
Permits, Fees, Inspections	$5,000–$10,000
Contingency (10–12%)	$20,000–$25,000

🏗 Final Expected Build Range:

☑ **$260,000–$350,000** (or around **$110–$135 per sq.ft.** finished)

This estimate **does NOT include** land purchase costs, major customizations, or owner upgrades like:

• High-end appliances

• Solar systems

• Pools, barns, or detached garages

Realistic lesson: Plan for your "bare minimum build" first, then stack upgrades carefully.

⚑ Contractor Red Flags You Must Watch For

Choosing the right contractor can **save you tens of thousands** — and just as importantly, it can save your sanity.

Here's what professional builders (and experienced clients) watch for when hiring:

▥ Red Flag #1: "We Don't Need a Written Contract."

No reputable builder works without clear written contracts specifying:

• Scope of work

• Materials included (and excluded)

• Payment terms

• Timeline and milestones

• Warranty policies

Why it matters:

A handshake is NOT a plan. Without a written contract, you lose all legal leverage if problems arise.

▥ Red Flag #2: Large Upfront Payment Demands

Typical contractor deposits range from **10–20%** of the total project value — enough to cover initial material orders and scheduling.

⚐ If someone demands **50% or more upfront**, it usually means:

• They're desperate for cash

• They don't have strong supplier credit

• They may walk away mid-project

Safe practice: Only pay progressively, based on completed, inspected work.

▥ Red Flag #3: "Trust Me, I'll Handle the Permits."

No professional contractor hides the permitting process from you.

You, as the property owner, should **see copies of all permits** issued and know what's being inspected and when.

Why it matters:

If work is performed without proper permits:

• Your Certificate of Occupancy can be denied

• You may face fines, insurance problems, or resale headaches later

▥ Red Flag #4: Vague Bids or "One-Line" Estimates

⚐ Example of a bad bid:

"Build 2400 SF house — labor and material — $250,000 total."

☑ A good bid is broken down by major stages:

• Slab

• Framing

• Roofing

- Windows/Doors
- Interior Finishes
- Mechanical Systems
- Final Trim/Touch-Up

Why it matters:

Without breakdowns, you have no way to compare quotes, spot inflated costs, or control upgrades later.

🎐 **Red Flag #5: "We Always Finish Early."**

It sounds great — but in construction, schedules slip because **reality happens**: rain, inspections, subcontractor delays, supply chain issues.

Professionals build in buffers.

When someone promises impossible deadlines, they're selling fantasy, not craftsmanship.

🧠 **Closing Thought: Budget With Eyes Open, Build With Confidence**

The best builders budget like engineers — clear, structured, and with backup plans.

Set your real budget based on necessity, not excitement.

Choose partners based on proof, not promises.

If you stay honest about your numbers and disciplined about your team, you'll not just build cheaper — you'll build smarter, safer, and more successfully.

GC OR DIY? HOW TO DECIDE AND WHAT TO EXPECT FROM BOTH.

One of the biggest decisions you'll face when building your barndominium is this:

Should you hire a General Contractor (GC) to manage the project, or should you act as your own builder (DIY Owner-Builder)?

Both paths have real advantages — and real risks.

The right choice isn't about pride, it's about matching your skills, time, and risk tolerance with the demands of your project.

In this section, we'll walk through a realistic view of **what each role really involves**, and how to make the best choice for your build, your budget, and your peace of mind.

🛠 **What a General Contractor (GC) Really Does**

A true GC is **a project manager, a scheduler, and a problem-solver** — not just a guy with a toolbelt.

When you hire a GC, you are paying for:

- **Coordination:** Managing subcontractors (framers, electricians, plumbers, etc.)
- **Permitting:** Handling inspections and paperwork with county officials.
- **Scheduling:** Ordering materials and sequencing crews correctly.

- **Problem Solving:** Dealing with weather delays, material shortages, and construction errors.
- **Warranty Management:** Fixing issues that come up during or after construction.

Typical GC Fee:

- 10%–20% of the total project cost (sometimes built into bids, sometimes added separately).

🦾 What DIY Owner-Building Involves

If you manage the build yourself, you take on **full responsibility** for:

- **Hiring and firing subs.**
- **Ordering and receiving materials.**
- **Coordinating inspections and permits.**
- **Problem solving daily.**
- **Managing construction timelines and budget flows.**

You save money (by avoiding GC markup fees), but you **pay in time, stress, and potential mistakes**.

Important:

Some banks will not finance a build unless a licensed GC is attached to the project.

Always check loan requirements first if financing.

🏗 Side-by-Side Comparison: GC vs DIY

Category	Hiring a GC	DIY Owner-Builder
Cost	+10%–20% of build	Potential savings of 10%–20% (if done well)
Control	Moderate (through GC)	Maximum (but full responsibility)
Time Commitment	Moderate (meetings, approvals)	Heavy (daily oversight required)
Risk of Delays/Errors	Lower (if GC is good)	Higher (if inexperienced)
Stress Level	Lower (delegate)	High (problem-solving is on you)
Loan Eligibility	Easier (lenders prefer GCs)	Possible restrictions or extra scrutiny
Warranty Protection	Stronger (GC managed)	Must negotiate with each subcontractor individually

📋 How to Decide Which Path Is Right for You

Ask yourself honestly:

- **Do you have 15–25 hours per week** available during the build phase?
- **Are you comfortable managing people**, making decisions quickly, and handling conflict?

- **Are you organized enough** to track budgets, schedules, inspections, and material deliveries?

- **Is your personality proactive or reactive** under pressure?

- **Do you have a trusted network of subcontractors**, or will you be hiring blind?

☑ If you answered **yes** to most of these — DIY might be a good path.

⚐ If you hesitated or answered **no** — you are likely better off hiring a GC.

There's no shame in either choice — the goal is to **get the home you want without losing your shirt or your sanity**.

🧠 **Pro Tips for Success Either Way**

If Hiring a GC:

- **Vet them thoroughly:** Check licensing, insurance, references, and current projects.

- **Get contracts in writing:** Scope, timelines, payment schedules.

- **Stay involved:** Visit the site often. Stay informed without micromanaging.

If DIY Owner-Building:

- **Hire a good construction lawyer** for basic contract templates.

- **Build a realistic timeline** — then add 20% extra for weather and unexpected issues.

- **Don't DIY everything:** Hire licensed pros for electrical, plumbing, HVAC to avoid inspections nightmares.

🚀 **Closing Thought:**

Build smart by **playing to your strengths**, not your fantasies.

Whether you hire a GC or DIY, success comes from **preparation, discipline, and the right expectations** — not luck.

Choose your role wisely. Your future home depends on it.

VISUAL CONSTRUCTION TIMELINE: WHAT HAPPENS WHEN AND IN WHAT ORDER

Building a barndominium isn't a free-for-all.

It's a **precisely ordered series of steps**, each depending on the successful completion of the phase before it.

Get the sequence right, and your project flows.

Miss a step, and you could face costly delays, inspection failures, or even structural problems down the line.

This section will walk you through a **realistic, field-tested construction timeline — what happens when, why the order matters**, and **where to stay sharp** as the build progresses.

🛠 **Phase 1: Land Prep and Foundation**

☑ **Timeline: 1–2 months (depending on land and permits)**

Step	Task	Notes
1	Land Clearing and Grading	Remove trees, debris, level site
2	Utility Pre-Installation	Water lines, septic rough-in, power lines
3	Soil Testing & Compaction (as needed)	Ensure site is stable and meets engineering specs
4	Foundation Layout and Forms	Slab preparation or pier layout
5	Pouring Foundation	Critical to allow proper curing time (7–28 days)

⚡ **Watchpoint:**

Before pouring, double-check plumbing sleeve placement. Errors here are extremely expensive to fix later.

🛠 **Phase 2: Structural Shell**

☑ **Timeline: 1–2 months**

Step	Task	Notes
6	Erect Framing (Steel/Post Frame/Wood)	Fast phase — can go up in days
7	Install Roofing	Metal panels or shingles
8	Install Siding/Exterior Walls	Metal or other finishes
9	Rough Door and Window Openings	Set for future installs

⚡ **Watchpoint:**

Ensure roof flashing and waterproofing details are inspected — 80% of future leaks start during rushed shell phases.

🛠 **Phase 3: Rough-Ins (Mechanical Systems)**

☑ **Timeline: 1–2 months**

Step	Task	Notes
10	Plumbing Rough-In	Water supply lines, drain lines
11	Electrical Rough-In	Wires, boxes, service panels
12	HVAC Rough-In	Ducts, vents, return air pathways
13	Low Voltage Systems	Internet, security, smart home wiring (optional)

⚡ **Watchpoint:**

Confirm all rough-ins pass preliminary inspections before proceeding.

Covering failed work with drywall = nightmare.

⚒ **Phase 4: Inspections and Insulation**

☑ **Timeline: 2–3 weeks**

Step	Task	Notes
14	Framing/Mechanical Inspections	Must pass before insulation
15	Install Insulation	Spray foam, batts, or hybrid systems

⚡ **Watchpoint:**

Spray foam locks errors inside walls forever — confirm all wiring/plumbing is correct before spraying.

⚒ **Phase 5: Interior Build-Out**

☑ **Timeline: 2–4 months**

Step	Task	Notes
16	Drywall Install	Tape, mud, sand
17	Interior Painting	Prime and finish coats
18	Flooring Installation	LVP, tile, engineered wood
19	Cabinet and Millwork Install	Kitchen and bath cabinetry, baseboards, trim
20	Appliance Install	Kitchen and laundry

⚡ **Watchpoint:**

Protect installed floors during cabinet work — careless crews can ruin $10,000 of flooring in a single day.

⚒ **Phase 6: Final Systems and Exterior Work**

☑ **Timeline: 1–2 months**

Step	Task	Notes
21	Final Electrical, Plumbing, HVAC Hookups	Fixtures, outlets, vents
22	Exterior Decks, Patios, Landscaping	Softscapes, driveways
23	Final Touch-Up Work	Paint, trim corrections, minor fixes
24	Final Inspections	Certificate of Occupancy issued
25	Move-In Ready!	Congratulations! 🎉

⚡ **Watchpoint:**

Final inspections often fail for minor issues (missing outlet covers, minor leaks) — run your own "mini-inspection" first.

▦ **Visual Flow Summary (Simple Diagram)**

Site Prep → Foundation → Shell → Rough-Ins → Insulation → Interior Build → Final Exterior/Systems → Inspection/Occupancy

🧠 **Closing Thought: Follow the Order, Win the Build**

Barndominium construction is a **marathon of sequencing**, not a sprint of random tasks.

If you understand the flow **before you ever break ground**, you can:

• Communicate better with contractors

• Catch errors early

• Keep your build on schedule and under budget

When you know what's coming next — you control the outcome.

Download Printable Construction Timeline Guide

Want a quick reference during your build?

Scan the QR code to download a **full-page printable version** of the construction timeline — perfect to bring to site meetings, hang in your workshop, or track your progress step-by-step.

ENERGY EFFICIENCY SYSTEMS: HVAC, INSULATION, SOLAR, WATER

Designing an energy-efficient barndominium isn't just good for the environment — it's smart economics.

Every dollar you invest upfront in the right systems pays you back month after month in lower utility bills, higher comfort, and longer system life.

But the key is choosing systems that actually make sense for **your climate, your usage, and your budget** — not just following trends.

In this section, we'll break down **the four essential pillars of energy efficiency** you should plan for from day one.

🧱 1. Insulation: The Foundation of Energy Efficiency

No system can compensate for a poorly insulated building.

Good insulation = lower HVAC costs, better comfort, and quieter interiors.

☑ Best Options for Barndominiums:

• **Closed-Cell Spray Foam (Top Tier Choice):**

○ Highest R-value per inch.

○ Air-seals and strengthens walls.

○ Best for steel-framed or post-frame structures.

• **Hybrid Systems (Budget-Friendly Option):**

○ Combine spray foam at critical points (roofline, rim joists) with batt insulation in walls.

○ Offers 80% of the benefit for 60% of the cost.

☑ Important Tip:

Always insulate **roof decks** properly — barndos have big open ceilings that leak energy fast if unprotected.

❄ 🔥 2. HVAC Systems: Heating, Cooling, and Air Quality

Barndominiums, with their open spaces and high ceilings, have special HVAC needs.

Oversized or improperly placed systems waste energy and leave cold/hot spots.

☑ Best HVAC Options:

• **Mini-Split Ductless Systems:**

○ Ideal for barndos up to ~2,500 sq. ft.

○ Zoned cooling and heating (no wasted energy).

○ Easier retrofitting, lower installation costs.

• **High-Efficiency Heat Pumps:**

○ Best in moderate to warm climates.

○ Provide heating and cooling from a single system.

• **Traditional Central HVAC (with Zoning):**

○ Necessary for larger barndos.

○ Always zone your great room separately from bedroom wings to avoid overworking the system.

☑ Important Tip:

Invest in **smart thermostats** (like Ecobee or Nest) — they optimize runtime and adjust for occupancy automatically.

☼ 3. Solar Energy Systems: Off-Grid or Grid-Tied

Solar can dramatically reduce lifetime costs, especially for rural barndos far from city utilities.

But it must be **designed realistically** — not idealistically.

☑ Realistic Solar Planning:

• **Grid-Tied Systems:**

○ Most common.

○ Provide energy savings and payback periods of 7–10 years depending on location.

• **Off-Grid Systems:**

○ Require substantial battery backup (Tesla Powerwall, etc.).

○ More costly upfront — best for remote builds where running utility lines is cost-prohibitive.

☑ Important Tip:

If planning solar later, **design roof pitches and orientations today** for maximum solar gain (typically south-facing in the U.S.).

⚿ 4. Water Systems: Efficiency Beyond Energy

Water management is often overlooked — but it's critical for barndominium efficiency and rural living.

☑ Key Strategies:

• **Tankless Water Heaters:**

○ Heat water only when needed.

○ Save 20–30% over traditional tank heaters.

○ Great for compact mechanical spaces.

• **Greywater Recycling (Advanced Option):**

○ Capture used water from showers, sinks, and laundry for irrigation.

○ Especially useful on large rural properties or off-grid sites.

• **Well and Septic Planning:**

○ Design for efficient pumping distances to reduce energy usage long-term.

○ Protect pressure tanks from extreme temperatures to extend system life.

☑ Important Tip:

Install low-flow fixtures where possible — but prioritize quality brands that maintain water pressure (cheap fixtures frustrate users and get removed).

▦ Quick Cost vs. Benefit Snapshot

System	Cost Estimate	Payback/Benefits
Spray Foam Insulation	$1.50–$3.00/sq.ft.	25–40% lower energy bills year-round
Mini-Split HVAC	$3,000–$6,000 per zone	Major savings on small/medium builds
Grid-Tied Solar	$15,000–$25,000 (after credits)	7–10 year payback, long-term ROI
Tankless Water Heater	$1,000–$2,000 installed	Saves 20–30% energy vs tank heaters

🧠 Closing Thought: Efficiency Is Designed, Not Installed

An energy-efficient barndominium isn't the result of buying expensive gadgets at the last minute — it's the result of **smart, integrated planning** from the very beginning.

Think systems working together, not isolated upgrades.

Every smart choice you make now builds a home that is **cheaper, cleaner, and more comfortable** for decades to come.

OFF-GRID OPTIONS AND PASSIVE DESIGN FOR LONG-TERM SAVINGS

For many barndominium builders, the dream goes beyond just owning a house — it's about creating **real independence**.

Energy freedom, water independence, and lower long-term costs aren't just wishful thinking anymore.

Off-grid systems and passive design principles are proven, accessible strategies that can make your barndominium more sustainable, resilient, and affordable to operate for decades.

In this section, we'll break down **practical off-grid options** and **passive design techniques** that you can apply whether you plan to go fully off-grid or just want maximum efficiency.

🔋 Off-Grid Living Options: Power, Water, and Waste

Going off-grid doesn't mean giving up comfort — it means designing smarter.

☑ **Power Systems:**

• **Solar Photovoltaic (PV) Panels + Battery Storage:**

○ Generates electricity independently from the grid.

○ Requires sufficient battery capacity (Tesla Powerwall, LG Chem, etc.) for nighttime and cloudy day use.

○ Hybrid systems (grid-tied with battery backup) offer flexibility and emergency security.

• **Backup Generators:**

○ Critical for true energy resilience.

○ Propane, diesel, or natural gas options depending on availability.

○ Auto-switching systems keep critical loads active during outages.

☑ **Water Systems:**

- **Private Wells:**

  ○ Deep wells (~150–300 feet typical) ensure consistent freshwater supply.

  ○ Plan for energy-efficient pumps and insulated pressure tanks.

- **Rainwater Harvesting:**

  ○ Collect and store rainwater for irrigation or even potable use (with proper filtration and treatment).

  ○ Especially useful in areas with seasonal droughts or poor municipal water access.

☑ **Waste Systems:**

- **Septic Systems:**

  ○ Standard solution for rural builds.

  ○ Ensure your system is properly sized for household size and future expansion.

- **Composting Toilets (Advanced Builds):**

  ○ Reduces blackwater waste.

  ○ Useful for accessory structures, workshops, or remote areas.

🏡 **Passive Design Strategies: Smarter Building, Less Energy Use**

Passive design is about **using natural forces** — sun, wind, shade — to your advantage so your home stays comfortable **without mechanical intervention**.

☑ **Key Passive Design Techniques:**

- **Site Orientation:**

  ○ Maximize **southern exposure** in colder climates to capture winter sun.

  ○ Minimize western window exposure in hotter climates to avoid late-day heat gain.

- **Window Placement and Sizing:**

  ○ Use larger windows on south-facing walls (with proper shading).

  ○ Minimize windows on east and west sides.

  ○ Use double or triple-pane windows for thermal efficiency.

- **Thermal Mass Usage:**

  ○ Concrete floors, interior brick, or stone features absorb daytime heat and slowly release it overnight, stabilizing indoor temperatures.

- **Cross-Ventilation:**

  ○ Position windows and doors to allow natural breezes to flow across living spaces.

  ○ Reduces air conditioning needs during mild seasons.

- **Overhangs and Shade Structures:**

  ○ Roof overhangs, covered patios, and pergolas reduce solar gain without blocking natural light.

  ○ Custom overhang sizing based on latitude optimizes seasonal performance.

- **Insulation Beyond Code:**

○ Go above minimum local code requirements, especially in roof and slab insulation.

○ A well-insulated envelope drastically improves passive performance.

▦ Off-Grid Cost Snapshot (Realistic Ballpark)

System	Typical Cost Range	Notes
Full Solar + Battery Setup	$30,000–$60,000	Depends on system size and backup needs
Deep Well Installation	$10,000–$20,000	Depth and geology impact costs
Septic System	$5,000–$15,000	Size and soil type dependent
Rainwater Harvesting System	$5,000–$12,000	Filtration adds to costs if potable

🧠 Practical Planning Tips for Off-Grid and Passive Builds

• Start with Efficiency:

Reduce loads first (lighting, appliances, insulation) before sizing expensive solar or generator systems.

• Plan Infrastructure Early:

Wells, septic, solar arrays, and battery banks all need space — plan your site layout with these in mind before you pour a slab.

• Design for Scalability:

Maybe you don't go fully off-grid today — but smart wiring, plumbing chases, and solar-ready roof angles keep your options open.

• Expect Maintenance:

Off-grid living isn't "set it and forget it." Pumps fail, inverters need replacement, batteries degrade over time. Budget for it.

🧠 Closing Thought:

True self-sufficiency isn't just about being disconnected from the grid — it's about designing your life and your home to thrive with fewer inputs.

Whether you go 100% off-grid or simply build smarter with passive design, the investment today delivers freedom, comfort, and security that lasts a lifetime.

THE "$25K MISTAKE" CHECKLIST: CRITICAL STEPS YOU CAN'T AFFORD TO MISS

Building a barndominium is exciting — but excitement without structure leads to expensive regrets.

Across hundreds of builds, there's a consistent pattern: **small missed steps early on lead to $10,000, $15,000, even $25,000+ mistakes** by the time construction is complete.

This checklist is your insurance policy.

Before you pour concrete, order trusses, or sign checks, review these critical steps carefully.

Ignoring just one could cost you more than the price of a brand-new truck.

🔥 **The Critical Pre-Construction Checklist**

☑️ **Land and Soil Verification Completed**

• Did you perform a soil test (geotechnical report) to confirm foundation suitability?

• Was your site graded properly with correct drainage planned?

☑️ **Zoning and Permitting Locked Down**

• Have you verified all local zoning regulations for your land?

• Do you have your building permit (not just an application started)?

• Are there setback, height, or special codes that could force redesigns?

☑️ **Utility Access Confirmed and Budgeted**

• Is power easily accessible?

• Do you have clear plans (and costs) for water, sewer/septic, gas, and internet?

• Have you budgeted realistic trenching and hookup fees?

☑️ **Realistic Total Build Cost Estimated (Not Just Shell)**

• Does your budget include slab, mechanicals (plumbing/electrical/HVAC), permits, finish work, contingency?

• Have you included 10%–15% for unexpected material/labor inflation?

☑️ **Contractor Vetting Completed**

• Have you verified insurance, licensing, references, and active job sites?

• Do you have multiple detailed bids (not just single-line quotes)?

☑️ **Engineering Plans Finalized**

• Is your structural engineer involved early to approve framing loads, wind ratings, and snow loads?

• Are your truss and slab designs stamped and ready?

☑️ **Detailed Material Specifications Agreed Upon**

• Roofing material type, insulation R-values, window performance specs — are they written into contracts?

• Is your siding thickness, panel gauge, and finish warranty confirmed?

☑️ **HVAC, Plumbing, and Electrical Rough-Ins Pre-Coordinated**

• Have you coordinated fixture locations with mechanical rough-ins?

• Are plumbing and electrical chases preplanned to avoid slab cutting?

☑️ **Insurance in Place Before Groundbreaking**

• Is your builder's risk insurance or self-build insurance active before the first shovel hits the dirt?

• Are liability policies checked and active for all contractors on site?

☑️ **Timeline Buffer Planned**

• Have you realistically padded your project timeline by 20% for weather, inspection, or supply delays?

⛏ The Top 5 "$25K Mistakes" (Real-World Examples)

1 Pouring a slab before final plumbing/electrical layout confirmation

○ ➜ Fix = Cut concrete later = $5,000–$15,000 extra.

2 Skipping soil tests on poor-quality lots

○ ➜ Fix = Over-engineered foundations or failed builds = $10,000–$50,000 disaster.

3 Missing rural access costs (power trenching, well drilling)

○ ➜ Surprise = $20,000+ unbudgeted expenses.

4 Hiring uninsured or poorly reviewed contractors

○ ➜ Fix = Lawsuits, code violations, or redoing entire phases.

5 Skipping engineered wind/snow load requirements

○ ➜ Result = Roof failures, denied insurance, structural rebuilds.

🧠 Closing Thought:

The real secret to saving $25,000 (or more) isn't getting lucky.

It's **doing the slow, disciplined work early**, while the stakes are low and mistakes are still cheap.

Check every box.

Ask every hard question.

Double-check every number.

Smart builders aren't paranoid — they're prepared.

That's how you build right the first time, with no expensive regrets.

CHAPTER 4
FINISH STRONG, LIVE FREE

Interior Design, Final Inspections, and Living the Life You Built

After months of planning, pouring, framing, wiring, and building, your project is finally entering its final phase.

This is where good projects either finish strong — or stumble to the end.

The last 10% of a barndominium build is deceptively important.

It's not just about picking paint colors or moving furniture.

It's about **critical inspections**, **final quality control**, **smart interior choices** that match the lifestyle you dreamed of — and setting up your home for decades of low-stress living.

In this chapter, you'll learn how to:

• Finalize your interior with practicality, efficiency, and comfort in mind — not just aesthetics.

• Prepare for inspections and certifications that legally open the door to your new life.

• Set up systems that simplify maintenance, boost efficiency, and protect your investment long term.

Finishing strong isn't just about completing construction.

It's about making sure your barndominium truly delivers the freedom, security, and satisfaction you set out to build.

Let's finish the right way — and start living free.

INTERIOR FINISHES: RUSTIC, MODERN, OR A BLEND OF BOTH

Choosing your interior finishes is where your barndominium truly transforms from a structure into a personal sanctuary.

This phase isn't just about style — it's about **creating durable, functional spaces** that match your lifestyle and stand the test of time.

Whether you're drawn to timeless rustic warmth, clean modern lines, or a thoughtful blend of both, the right finishes make all the difference.

🌲 Rustic Charm: Warm, Natural, and Inviting

Rustic interiors emphasize **authenticity and comfort**.

Natural materials, textured finishes, and earth-toned palettes set a relaxed, welcoming tone.

Typical rustic elements:

• Exposed wood beams and trusses

• Shiplap walls or natural wood paneling

• Stone fireplaces and hearths

• Matte black or oil-rubbed bronze fixtures

• Wide-plank hardwood or wood-look flooring

• Neutral, earthy color schemes: taupe, sand, sage, slate gray

Rustic interiors feel especially at home in barndominiums, enhancing the "homestead" atmosphere while still feeling fresh and refined.

🏠 Modern Minimalism: Clean, Bright, and Functional

Modern finishes bring a **streamlined, airy, and highly functional** feel to barndominiums.

They highlight open spaces, natural light, and simplicity — perfect for maximizing every square foot.

Key modern elements:

• Smooth walls in soft whites, light grays, or muted tones

• Sleek metal or minimalist wood fixtures

• Black or brushed metal accents

• Oversized glass doors and high windows

• Polished concrete or luxury vinyl plank (LVP) flooring

• Minimalist cabinetry with clean lines and hidden hardware

Modern interiors work especially well if you're building a barndo to be energy-efficient, low-maintenance, and future-forward.

🔥 The Best of Both Worlds: Rustic-Modern Fusion

The majority of today's successful barndominium designs blend rustic and modern elements **seamlessly** — creating homes that feel both cozy and cutting-edge.

How to achieve a rustic-modern balance:

• Pair exposed wood beams with smooth, neutral walls

• Mix reclaimed wood with clean-lined modern furniture

• Install black-framed windows and minimalist metal light fixtures over rustic hardwood floors

• Combine matte finishes with subtle natural textures

• Use stone or brick focal points within an otherwise simple, bright space

This hybrid style delivers the best of both worlds:

✔ Visual warmth without feeling heavy

✔ Clean living spaces without feeling sterile

✎ **Choosing Finishes That Last**

No matter your style, barndominiums demand **smart material choices** for longevity:

• **Flooring:** Opt for durable options like engineered hardwood, luxury vinyl plank (LVP), or sealed concrete.

• **Cabinetry:** Solid wood or high-quality composite materials resist warping and damage better than budget alternatives.

• **Walls and Ceilings:** Use moisture-resistant drywall where needed (especially in kitchens, bathrooms, and laundry areas).

• **Fixtures:** Choose finishes that can withstand heavy use and rural environments (matte black, brushed nickel, bronze).

A beautiful interior isn't just about visual impact — it's about choosing elements that look great **and** perform well for years with minimal upkeep.

🧠 **Pro Tip:**

Plan your interior finish selections early, ideally during the framing stage.

Why?

Because certain design choices — like ceiling height, lighting placement, or window sizing — **directly affect the final look and feel** of your spaces.

Good planning now avoids costly rework later.

Visual Inspiration: Realistic Design Renderings

To help you visualize the possibilities for your own barndominium, the following design renderings show examples of interior finishes that combine smart planning, durable materials, and timeless style.

Each space captures a different balance between rustic warmth and modern simplicity — offering you inspiration for creating a home that's not only **beautiful**, but **built for real life**.

PASSING INSPECTION: WHAT THEY'LL CHECK AND HOW TO PREPARE

No matter how beautiful your barndominium looks, you can't move in — or insure it — until it officially passes final inspections.

Building inspections are designed to **protect your safety**, **verify code compliance**, and **certify workmanship**.

They're not something to rush or ignore.

The good news?

If you understand what inspectors focus on — and plan for it early — you can avoid costly rework, project delays, and frustration.

Here's how to approach it like a professional.

What Inspectors Will Check

While every jurisdiction has slight differences, most final inspections include these key areas:

• **Structural Integrity:**

Inspectors check that the foundation, framing, roofing, and load-bearing structures meet local building codes and engineered specifications.

• Electrical Systems:

Wiring must be correctly installed and safely connected, with proper breaker sizing, GFCI outlets where required, and no exposed junctions.

• Plumbing Systems:

All water lines, drains, and vents must be properly installed, leak-free, and vented according to code.

• HVAC Installation:

Heating, ventilation, and air conditioning systems must be safely installed with proper clearances, airflow, and energy efficiency compliance.

• Insulation and Energy Efficiency:

Depending on your location, inspectors may verify insulation R-values, air sealing, and any special energy code requirements.

• Fire Safety:

Working smoke detectors, carbon monoxide detectors (if required), fire-rated walls between attached garages and living areas, and safe egress routes must be present.

• Site and Drainage:

Inspectors confirm that the final grading around your barndominium slopes correctly to direct water away from the foundation.

• General Code Compliance:

Miscellaneous items like handrails, stair dimensions, address signage, minimum window sizes for bedrooms (egress), and safe deck construction will also be reviewed.

How to Prepare for a Smooth Final Inspection

Passing the first time isn't about luck — it's about **organization and attention to detail**.

Here's how to prepare smartly:

• Schedule early.

As soon as final finishes are underway, contact your local inspection office to schedule your final inspections. Avoid waiting until the last minute.

• Do your own mini-inspections first.

Walk through your home using a checklist to spot obvious issues: missing outlet covers, loose fixtures, leaking faucets, unfinished stair railings, missing smoke alarms.

• Confirm all paperwork is ready.

Have all necessary permits, engineer letters (if required), septic or well approvals, and energy compliance certificates available onsite.

• Clean the job site.

A clean, accessible space shows professionalism and makes it easy for inspectors to do their job without tripping over tools or debris.

• **Be present (or send a knowledgeable representative).**

Someone who understands the project must be available to answer questions, locate documents, and clarify details if necessary.

🧠 **Pro Tip:**

Document your build as you go.

Take photos of plumbing, wiring, insulation, and framing *before drywall goes up*.

If an inspector questions something they can't physically see, you'll have proof ready — saving time, arguments, and money.

By treating inspections as **an essential part of your success — not an obstacle** — you'll stay in control of your project timeline, budget, and ultimate move-in date.

Remember:

A great build isn't just about beauty — it's about building **right**.

REAL SUCCESS STORIES: WHAT REAL BARNDOMINIUM OWNERS LEARNED THE HARD WAY

Building a barndominium isn't just a technical project — it's a life-changing investment.

And like any transformative journey, the best lessons often come through real-world experience.

Fortunately, you don't have to make all the mistakes yourself.

These families once stood exactly where you are now — full of excitement, plans, and a few unknowns.

Here are their stories — what went right, what went wrong, and what you can learn to finish your own project stronger, smarter, and with fewer regrets.

🧱 The Martins — Budgeting Saved Their Dream

The Situation:

The Martins sold their suburban home to fund their dream of a custom barndominium on five acres. Their planning was solid — until lumber prices spiked 18% midway through framing.

The Smart Move:

They had reserved 15% of their total project budget for unexpected expenses.

The Outcome:

Instead of halting construction or borrowing more money, they absorbed the extra $18,000 without stress or delays.

🏁 **Lesson Learned:**

Always build a real contingency fund into your budget.

Market prices, supply shortages, and project surprises are not "if" — they're "when."

⚠ The Coopers — Rushing the Slab Cost Them Thousands

The Situation:

The Coopers, eager to move in before winter, pushed their contractor to pour their foundation slab right after a week of heavy rain.

The Fallout:

Within months, cracks appeared across their slab, floors began shifting, and moisture seeped into walls — requiring $14,000 in repairs.

⚑ Lesson Learned:

Never rush your foundation.

Good soil compaction, dry conditions, and patience at this phase are critical for long-term stability.

🗄 The Walkers — Storage Regrets That Cost More Later

The Situation:

The Walkers loved open-concept living and intentionally minimized closets, pantry space, and utility rooms to save money and keep their floor plan "clean."

The Reality:

Within the first year, their dream space felt cramped and chaotic. They ultimately built a detached garage for extra storage — at double the cost compared to adding it during initial construction.

⚑ Lesson Learned:

Design for daily life, not magazine covers.

Storage and utility space aren't luxuries — they are essential parts of real-world living.

🌡 The Reynoldses — HVAC Shortcuts = Comfort Disasters

The Situation:

Trying to keep costs down, the Reynoldses hired the cheapest HVAC subcontractor they could find and accepted a "basic" setup without zoning.

The Consequence:

Poor airflow left parts of their home nearly unlivable during summer, while energy bills skyrocketed. They eventually had to replace the system, losing over $12,000.

⚑ Lesson Learned:

Don't skimp on HVAC.

Comfort, efficiency, and utility costs depend on good system design from the beginning.

📶 The Ellisons — Rural Internet Almost Ruined Their Dream

The Situation:

The Ellisons, remote workers, assumed internet service would be simple to access in their rural Missouri location.

The Oversight:

Only after moving dirt and pouring concrete did they discover the nearest high-speed line was four miles away. After failed satellite and hotspot attempts, they had to install costly equipment.

🏁 **Lesson Learned:**

Verify infrastructure early.

Water, power, septic, and internet must be part of your land-buying checklist — not afterthoughts.

🧰 The Harrisons — DIY Burnout and Hidden Costs

The Situation:

Experienced DIYers, the Harrisons planned to handle most of the build themselves to save money.

The Problem:

Six months in, decision fatigue, physical exhaustion, and a family emergency slowed their progress. In the end, they hired out more work than planned — spending nearly the same as if they'd used a general contractor from the beginning.

🏁 **Lesson Learned:**

Honor your limits.

DIY builds demand serious stamina, organization, and support. Know when to delegate — your health and finances depend on it.

🏠 The Rodriguezes — Site Planning Saved Their Home

The Situation:

Aware they were building in a low-lying Texas area, the Rodriguezes invested $7,500 upfront in engineered grading and a raised slab foundation.

The Outcome:

Two years later, when historic flooding hit their area, every neighbor's home took damage — except theirs.

🏁 **Lesson Learned:**

Spend smart on land prep and elevation.

Drainage, grading, and foundation planning are invisible investments — until disaster strikes.

🔍 What These Stories Reveal

These aren't extreme outliers.

They are common, real-world challenges that affect thousands of barndominium builds every year.

Successful owners all share one mindset:

• They planned for surprises.

• They respected the fundamentals — site, structure, systems.

• They built for real life, not just idealized dreams.

You don't have to learn the hard way.

You just have to learn smart.

✅ **Quick Action Checklist: Learn From Experience**

Before your build begins, check these critical lessons off:

• [ ] Reserve a 10–15% budget buffer for the unexpected.

• [ ] Prioritize proper soil, slab prep, and drainage before anything else.

• [ ] Include real-world storage and functional spaces in your plan.

• [ ] Vet HVAC installers carefully; insist on quality and zoning.

• [ ] Confirm infrastructure access — water, septic, power, and internet — at land purchase.

• [ ] Be realistic about your capacity to DIY versus the demands of managing a major build.

• [ ] Protect your property with smart site engineering from the start.

🚀 **Closing Thought:**

These families didn't fail — they adapted, persevered, and finished their builds stronger for the lessons they learned.

By standing on their shoulders, you get to build smarter from the very first nail — and create a barndominium that delivers on your dreams without unnecessary detours.

LONG-TERM MAINTENANCE AND UPGRADES TO PROTECT YOUR INVESTMENT

A well-built barndominium isn't just a beautiful place to live — it's a **major financial asset**.

Protecting that investment doesn't happen automatically.

It takes **simple, regular maintenance** and **smart upgrades** that extend the life of your structure, preserve energy efficiency, and increase future resale value.

In this section, we'll focus on the real-world strategies that keep your barndo strong, efficient, and valuable for decades — without overwhelming you.

🧹 **Essential Annual Maintenance Checklist**

✅ **Roof and Gutter Inspection:**

• Inspect for loose fasteners, sealant wear, minor leaks, and debris buildup.

• Clear gutters and downspouts every spring and fall to prevent water damage.

✅ **Exterior Siding Check:**

• Wash metal siding with low-pressure water to remove dirt, mildew, and chemicals.

• Touch up scratches or chips in metal coatings before rust develops.

✅ **Foundation and Grading Inspection:**

• Walk the perimeter looking for cracks, settling, or water pooling near the slab.

• Regrade soil or extend downspouts if water isn't flowing away correctly.

☑ HVAC System Service:

• Replace filters every 1–3 months.

• Schedule professional HVAC tune-ups before winter and summer seasons.

☑ Plumbing and Water Systems:

• Test water pressure.

• Inspect visible pipes for signs of leaks or corrosion.

• Flush water heaters annually to remove sediment buildup.

☑ Septic System Check (if applicable):

• Pump septic tanks every 2–5 years depending on system size and usage.

• Monitor drain field health — soggy areas may signal problems.

☑ Interior Caulking and Sealing:

• Check around windows, doors, and plumbing fixtures.

• Recaulk as needed to maintain energy efficiency and prevent moisture intrusion.

🔧 Long-Term Smart Upgrades to Consider

Even if your barndominium is new today, a few smart investments over time can **boost comfort, lower energy bills, and add serious resale value**.

☑ Solar System Additions:

• Install photovoltaic panels with battery backup once your energy use patterns are clear.

☑ Upgrading Insulation in Critical Areas:

• Blow-in attic insulation to maintain R-values after settling.

☑ Energy-Efficient Window Replacements:

• Future upgrade to triple-pane windows for superior thermal performance if needed.

☑ Smart Home System Integration:

• Add remote lighting control, leak detection sensors, and HVAC automation to save energy and protect the home during absences.

☑ Landscape Grading Improvements:

• Upgrade drainage patterns and install low-maintenance native plant landscaping to reduce erosion and maintenance effort.

☑ Outbuilding Construction (Workshops, Guest Houses):

• Expand functional spaces to enhance property versatility and future resale appeal.

▦ Protecting Resale Value

Even if you plan to live in your barndo for life, circumstances change.

Keeping your home **well-maintained and energy-efficient**:

- Commands higher resale prices
- Attracts better buyers (especially those looking for rural homes)
- Protects you from expensive emergency repairs later

Maintenance isn't a cost — it's an investment multiplier.

🧠 **Pro Tip:**

Document all maintenance and upgrades.

Keep a digital binder or folder with receipts, service records, warranty certificates, and inspection reports.

When it's time to refinance, resell, or claim insurance benefits, your organized records will save time, stress, and thousands of dollars.

HOW TO MAKE YOUR BARNDOMINIUM FEEL LIKE HOME FROM DAY ONE

After all the months of planning, building, budgeting, and inspections, it's easy to cross the threshold of your finished barndominium and feel… a little overwhelmed.

An empty, echoing house — no matter how well built — doesn't automatically feel like home.

Home is created intentionally.

It's built by **small decisions** that reflect your life, your priorities, and your comfort.

Here's how you can make your new space feel truly yours — right from the first day.

🏗️ **1. Start With Comfort, Not Perfection**

Forget trying to "finish" every room immediately.

Focus on the **critical daily comfort zones** first:

- Set up your main bedroom completely (curtains, bedding, lighting, storage)
- Assemble a simple, working living room or family area
- Install essential kitchen items even if not fully decorated

Living comfortably **comes before** full decorating.

Comfort fuels momentum.

🖼️ **2. Personalize Early (Even Small Touches Matter)**

A few early personal touches make a huge psychological difference:

- Hang 2–3 framed family photos
- Place a familiar piece of furniture (even if temporary)
- Add a cozy throw, favorite lamp, or a beloved piece of art

Even small anchors of familiarity turn a house into a home faster than waiting for "perfect" setups.

3. Bring Life In (Literally)

Natural elements instantly soften large, fresh spaces:

• Place a few potted plants near windows

• Add a herb garden starter in the kitchen

• Arrange a simple outdoor seating area — even a small patio table and chairs

Greenery, sunlight, and airflow make new spaces feel vibrant and alive — not sterile.

4. Define Outdoor Spaces Early

Even minimal outdoor setups — like:

• A firepit area

• Basic garden beds

• A hammock or porch swing

— immediately extend your living area and **connect you emotionally to the land** you built your dream on.

Barndominium living isn't just about the structure.

It's about **the space around it, too**.

5. Give Yourself Permission to Grow Into It

Don't pressure yourself to have everything perfect by move-in week.

Great homes evolve over time, layer by layer.

By focusing first on comfort, familiarity, and the spaces you actually use daily, you build a home that supports your real life — not just a showroom fantasy.

Closing Thought:

Your barndominium isn't just a shelter — it's the basecamp for the life you're choosing to live.

Build daily comfort.

Celebrate small victories.

Let your home evolve with you.

From day one, you're not just moving into a building — **you're stepping into the life you built with your own vision, hands, and heart.**

A LOOK FORWARD: LEGACY LIVING, RESALE VALUE, AND FINANCIAL FREEDOM

Building a barndominium isn't just a project.

It's a legacy move.

By investing the time, discipline, and vision to create a customized, efficient, and durable home, you're planting seeds that will continue paying dividends for decades to come — financially, emotionally, and personally.

In this final section, we'll look forward to the long-term rewards you've built into your life and your property.

🏡 Legacy Living: More Than Just a House

A well-built barndominium isn't just where you live — it's a foundation for a lifestyle:

• Family headquarters:

A home large enough, flexible enough, and practical enough to host generations, hobbies, businesses, and new dreams.

• Self-sufficiency:

Systems like private wells, solar power, efficient heating and cooling, and passive design mean more control and lower ongoing costs.

• Security:

Owning a rural, fully functional property offers a level of independence and resilience few suburban homes can match.

Legacy living means building a place that doesn't just serve you today — it supports your family for generations.

📈 Resale Value: A Growing Market

Barndominiums are no longer a niche idea.

Across the U.S., demand for flexible, energy-efficient rural homes is growing rapidly — and with it, resale values.

☑ Well-maintained barndominiums in desirable areas often:

• Sell faster than traditional homes

• Command higher per-square-foot prices due to land, space, and durability

• Attract a wider range of buyers: remote workers, retirees, homesteaders, hobby farmers, and entrepreneurs

☑ Your early smart choices — energy efficiency, practical layouts, durable materials — will continue to pay off when (or if) you ever decide to sell.

Barndominiums built with quality and foresight **don't depreciate — they appreciate.**

💰 Financial Freedom: Lower Costs, Greater Control

Owning a barndominium built the right way offers real financial freedom compared to traditional suburban mortgages:

• Lower property taxes (in many rural areas)

• Lower maintenance costs due to durable materials and efficient systems

• Lower utility bills thanks to insulation, solar, passive design, and smart systems

• No HOA fees or heavy urban regulation costs

• Potential income: Renting out extra space, building detached units, operating workshops or home businesses directly from your property

The result?

You keep more of your hard-earned money — and you stay in control of your home and future.

🧠 Final Thought:

Your barndominium is more than just a home.

It's a statement:

That your life, your dreams, and your independence are worth building intentionally.

By making smart decisions now — planning, building, maintaining, and evolving — you haven't just created shelter.

You've built freedom, security, and legacy.

And that's the ultimate reward of living life on your own terms.

GLOSSARY

Barndominium (Barndo):

A structure that combines barn-style architecture with residential living spaces, often using steel or post-frame construction methods.

Building Envelope:

The physical separation between the interior and exterior environments of a building, including walls, roof, and foundation.

Closed-Cell Spray Foam:

A high-performance insulation material that provides a vapor barrier, high R-value, and structural reinforcement.

Contingency Fund:

Extra money set aside (typically 10–15% of the total budget) to cover unexpected expenses during construction.

Framing:

The structural skeleton of a building, made from steel, wood, or other materials, that supports walls, floors, and roof.

General Contractor (GC):

A licensed professional responsible for coordinating and supervising all aspects of a construction project, from hiring subcontractors to managing permits and inspections.

Greywater:

Gently used water from bathroom sinks, showers, tubs, and washing machines that can be recycled for non-potable uses like irrigation.

HVAC:

Heating, Ventilation, and Air Conditioning — the systems that regulate indoor climate and air quality.

Insulation R-Value:

A measurement of how well insulation resists heat flow; higher R-values mean better thermal performance.

Mini-Split System:

A ductless HVAC system ideal for efficient heating and cooling of specific zones within a building.

Passive Solar Design:

A construction approach that uses building orientation, window placement, materials, and insulation to naturally regulate indoor temperatures without mechanical systems.

Permits:

Official government approvals required before certain construction activities can begin, ensuring compliance with building codes and zoning regulations.

Post-Frame Construction:

A method using widely spaced, heavy timber or steel posts instead of traditional framing, allowing for wide-open interior spaces with fewer load-bearing walls.

Punch List:

A document created at the end of a construction project listing work that does not conform to contract specifications and must be corrected before final payment.

Septic System:

An underground wastewater treatment structure commonly used in rural areas without centralized sewer systems.

Solar Photovoltaic (PV) System:

A system that converts sunlight into electricity using solar panels mounted on the roof or ground.

Structural Engineer:

A licensed professional who designs and certifies load-bearing structures to ensure they are safe and compliant with building codes.

Underlayment:

A water-resistant or waterproof layer installed beneath roofing materials to provide extra protection from moisture intrusion.

Well Water System:

A private water supply system that draws groundwater for domestic use, typically including a pump, pressure tank, and filtration system.

Zoning Regulations:

Municipal or county rules that control land use, including what types of buildings can be constructed and how land can be developed.

ABOUT THE AUTHOR

Cole Bennett is a lifelong builder, rural property owner, and advocate for smart, sustainable living.

After overseeing multiple custom home builds — including his family's own off-grid barndominium project — Cole realized how overwhelming and costly the building process can be for first-time owners.

Drawing from years of real-world experience in land development, project management, and hands-on construction, he created this guide to help everyday families take control of their dreams without breaking the bank.

Through practical strategies, honest advice, and real-world examples, Cole empowers readers to build smarter, save thousands, and live the independent, self-sufficient lifestyle they've always wanted.

When he's not designing barndominiums or helping others plan their projects, Cole enjoys working on his rural property, restoring old tools, and teaching his kids the value of building something with your own hands.

Made in the USA
Coppell, TX
08 June 2025

50440487R00050